A Bride's Nightie

The ups and downs of Tony Thorpe

by

Tony Thorpe

First published in 2014 via iBooks

This edition published in 2021

www.tony-thorpe.co.uk

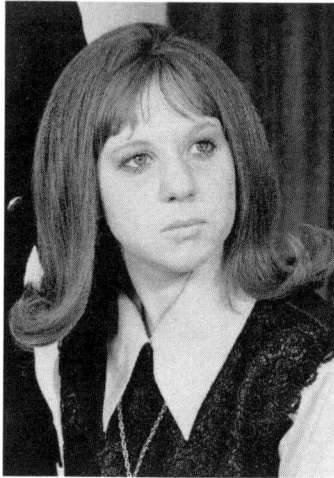

In loving memory of

Shirley Thorpe

1950-2013

Introduction

Have you heard the one about the musician who couldn't tell an $E7^{\#}9$ from a $Bb13^{b}9_{b}5$?   There's students of harmony pissing themselves over that one.

I started writing this book because people kept telling me 'you should write a book, you' and I got fed up explaining why no one would publish it. Publishers are like record companies, I said, only interested in 'star' biographies like Peter Andre's or Mick Hucknell's (sarcasm, come on in). But then I thought, wait a minute - if I pack the book with tales of my drug-fuelled sex orgies they're sure to go for it. Then I thought, wait a minute - I haven't had any. I'd have to make them up, and then it would be a novel, not an autobiography, and I like autobiographies. I read lots of them, usually the ones about the people who wrote them. Then I thought wait a minute, I know quite a lot about me, I could write one of them. So I did and d'you know what? Turns out I'm fascinating. Who'd have thunk that? Now if only I was Peter Andre I could get the fucking thing published.

This is going to sound strange, but I don't recognise myself in mirrors. I know the face – God knows I've seen it often enough - but it's not me. It doesn't feel like me in any way, shape or form, and it comes as a shock every time I see it. It's not a vanity thing, though it would be nice to see something attractive for a change. I genuinely expect to see someone quite different looking back at me. We may all feel like that, I suppose, but I've never heard anyone else mention it.

To begin at the beginning…

I was born right smack dab in the middle of the City of London in Bart's Hospital, giving me a God-given right to eff and blind. It's my cultural heritage. Cockneys are renowned for their fruity, creative language, which is why 'Minder' and 'Only Fools and Horses' are a damned sight more accurate than 'EastEnders' ever was. Of course London hardly exists any more as wave after wave of development has obliterated its architecture and character, but the same can be said of every sizeable town in England.

I remember when they created places like Basildon; 'new' towns they called them and fine as long as they were new. (Actually not fine, 'cause they looked bloody awful even then). But then we started turning old towns into 'new' towns by tearing them down and replacing them all with Basildon, an act of barbarism that has left us with nothing but soul-destroying nonentities. Then we wonder why we have no sense of community. All this was done in the name of 'town planning', an activity which consists of people in suits lining their pockets by allowing property developers to do what they like for personal gain and bollocks to the rest of us. Very uplifting. I grieve when I see some European towns and cities looking exactly as they did two hundred years ago – no Tescos, no McDonalds – places like Prague for instance, or just about any town in Italy. Then I look at Leeds or Blackburn. What is it about the English that makes us so philistine? I mean, they must have greedy developers and bribable planners in Italy, why doesn't *Florence* look like Basildon?

I became aware of all this early on because the first places to suffer were theatres. We can still appreciate the wonder of them because we still have a few places like Frank Matcham's glorious London Palladium, but there were places like the Palladium everywhere once, works of art that were bulldozed in droves so we could replace them with cheap concrete warehouses. We did the same to all those art deco cinemas too, and for what? To make someone in a suit more money. The thing with this sort of destruction is that there ain't no going back; once it's gone it's gone and we're all the poorer for it. But that's us I suppose; we've always let people in suits walk all over us for personal gain. Or do we genuinely not give a fuck?

So, I was born in London in 1945 as part of the 'end of war' celebrations. My mum, Angie, was pure-blood Italian whose parents had come over here to nick all our jobs off us; my dad, Fred, about as English as you can get. These names date me as sure as my DOB as hardly anyone these days would call anyone Fred and Angie. They'd be Frederick and Angela now, the legacy of Thatcher's insistence that we're all middle class. You even hear people calling their kids Thomas or Rebecca or Asiatica or Paramedic in Morrison's these days, a move I couldn't possibly disapprove of more.

Not that I have anything against Morrison's (their kitchen towels are my favourites), it's just that there's a warmth and familiarity about shortened names that makes us more human and less officious. For my own part, I hate to be called 'Anthony'. I hardly even acknowledge it as my name. Only the dreaded 'authorities' and my doctor call me 'Anthony' and I've told him God knows how many times. I don't even like 'Tony' to be honest – it's 'Tone' as far as I'm concerned, which is, let's face it, a damned fine name for a musician. Where was I? Oh yeah…

My early environment consisted of Harringay (old spelling, used deliberately) and Wood Green, my earliest playground was Finsbury Park which was opposite my parents' shops (or vice-versa) in Green Lanes - a greengrocer's first (my dad's trade) then a hardware shop two doors along.

Everybody knows about Italian families, I'm sure, so it should come as no surprise that it was the Italian side of the family (the Cairas) that dominated my childhood and I had two aunts and five uncles around me in shifts. (When I was very young there was Auntie Pip, too, a vague figure who was famous in the family because she once gave a throat sweet to the great Italian tenor Benjamino Gigli when he sang at the Italian church in Shoreditch, but I just remember her as an old lady who dressed in black, spoke hardly any English and taught everybody else how to cook Italian food, a legacy I'm glad to say filtered all the way down to my wife).

They'd all had it hard growing up as immigrants and the children of immigrants in Hoxton and were hard as nails themselves as a result. People now complain about street violence, quite rightly, but my mum told me that back then when the local mob came looking for the Italian boys the street would get wind of it, the shopkeepers would shut up shop, barricade the doors and windows and wait while the two opposing forces went at it outside with knives, cut-throat razors and bike chains. Only when it was all over would they open up, drag the bodies out of the road, sweep the blood into the gutters and start trading again. She never mentioned the police, my mum – presumably they had more sense than to get involved.

Thus the Italians gained a certain reputation, and as a result all my uncles knew the Kray Twins, Ronnie and Reggie – they even drank in my uncle Arnold's pub occasionally – and one of uncle Ern's best mates was Kray associate Mad Frankie Fraser, who Ern insists was 'a nice bloke', so you get the picture. Another of Ern's mates, incidentally, ran Rossi's Ice Cream business and had a son called Francis.

Me, I took after my old man. He'd grown up in the same area but was pacifist by nature, a real sweetheart. He never hit me (well, none of them did), he'd gain my compliance by saying we'd be 'bad friends' if I let him down and I loved him too much to do that. Neither he nor my mum showed any affection of the cuddling persuasion, nor did the rest of the family, but then cuddling wasn't 'in' in those days so I never felt hard done-by. In fact I couldn't have felt better cared-for.

NB: Both my dad's parents were gone by the time I was born, as was my mum's mum, so I only had one grandparent – Vincent – but I hardly ever saw him and after fifty-odd years he still hardly spoke any English anyway. Bloody immigrants, can't even be bothered to learn the fucking language.

I only remember my dad ever giving me one of those 'lesson for life' talks, and it went back to when he was in the Navy during the war. He wasn't in it long enough to see any action as he was allowed out on compassionate grounds because my mum's nerves were in pieces (which I reckon makes perfect sense if you've had people dropping bloody great bombs on you night after night). He'd done officer training in the Navy and he told me that the real officers, the privileged 'silver spoon' variety who'd gone to public school and become officers straight away, had been warm and friendly towards him, called him Fred and so on.

It was the NCOs who had come up through the ranks, he said, who threw their weight around and acted as if they were better than you. You may well recognise this from your own place of work, because I've noticed since that it's a pretty general state of affairs. Both these lessons were to affect the rest of my life one way or another, because I inherited my dad's understanding of the class system and my mum's nerves. One of which I've found useful.

I don't remember my mum or my dad ever having hobbies or pastimes or interests. They didn't read much or play any music, just listened to the radio (sorry, 'wireless') and watched TV (it was just 9 inches in those days, and I'm talking about the TV here. 9 inches and black and white, and I'm still talking about the TV).

This wasn't because they were thick. My old man scored over 160 in his Navy IQ test and he'd worked his way up from extreme poverty to become his own boss, which you don't do unless you've got something about you. It was because they were shopkeepers and shopkeepers had very little time to themselves. Hardly a day off, never mind a week, and they were too knackered by closing time to do anything much but cook, eat and sleep. It had ever been thus, and I had no interest in the family business. Mum went to church every Sunday, dad didn't (well he did, but only to chauffeur me mum) but I reckon he was one of the most Christian men I ever knew.

This being just about post-war there was still rationing but I don't remember us ever going short of anything. I reckon this was down to two things – my dad being a shopkeeper, and hence well in with all purveyors of consumables including the butcher, and my uncles' associates on the fringes of crime. Not so much hard-core villains, but the 'black market' brigade who frequently found things that had fallen off the backs of lorries, and they were very insecure in those days, lorries, especially round the back.

It seems weird now, but there were no shopping malls or supermarkets back then, only shops and the occasional shady character with insecure lorry connections. I seem to remember that Big Rena got anything she needed urgently by sending me to Baldetti's, a sort of counter at the back of a yard just around the corner from her house that kept a well-stocked store of bread rolls and cheese. How we managed without Tesco is beyond me, but we not only managed, we always ate well.

My formal education (yes, I had one) started at St Mary's Priory in Tottenham, a Catholic primary school run and staffed by nuns. Steeped in real traditional Catholicism, it preached and practised the very best kind of Christianity and I never saw any trouble there, nor any punishment more severe than 'go and stand in the corridor'. The teaching was great, I felt perfectly valued, and as a result I did well there.

NB: I don't know why I remember it so clearly, but when I started learning to read I was startled to find that 'potato' started with a P. They had always been 'bataters' in our neck of the woods. I also remember getting a funny look when the teacher asked if anyone knew what the phrase 'tit for tat' meant and I confidently volunteered the answer 'hat, sister' as that was what my dad called it. Apparently it had another meaning I was unaware of.

Away from school my early home life was pretty uneventful. I didn't make friends easily and being an only child meant that I spent quite a lot of time on my own, but I don't remember being too bothered about it and I preferred the company of adults to kids anyway. They had much more interesting things to talk about and I enjoyed listening to them.

There was always a stack of the family's 78rpm records around and I played all of them over and over again on a wind-up gramophone (they told me it was electric but it was just a wind-up, get it? Please yourself) - a couple of Bing Crosby's (including 'The Waiter and the Porter and the Upstairs Maid' with Jack Teagarden and Mary Martin –

fabulosa), a couple of Disney things I'd been given as presents and a load of 1930s and 40s English dance band records 'with vocal chorus'. I loved them all, but my favourites were probably 'Jollity Farm' by Leslie Sarony and 'When You Wish Upon a Star' from Disney's 'Snow White'. All those orchestral harmonies, beautiful.

Then when I was about seven (I think) my mum and dad started taking me to weekly variety at the Finsbury Park Empire (another Frank Matcham masterpiece and a perfect example of a No 1 theatre in the Moss Empires chain) thus beginning my love affair with theatre and show business. They'd had a regular weekly box at the theatre for years and I fell in love with the whole kit and caboodle instantly – the mahogany woodwork, the gold-leafed plasterwork, the massive curtains, the red velvet upholstery, the shape of the stalls and circles, the band in the pit, the acts on the stage, the sounds, the laughter, the applause, everything.

I didn't realise it at the time but weekly variety was on its last legs by then. The disruption of the war and the combined challenges of cinema, TV and radio (sorry, 'wireless') were all pulling the rug from under it and within a few years it was on its arse. It had probably run its course, I guess, but we lost something valuable and that's a shame. (Some years later, just before it was demolished, the old Empire was used as the setting for the 'let's do the show right here' section of Cliff Richard's movie 'The Young Ones' and it's heart-breaking to see it in that state. Better than not seeing it at all, though, I suppose). My mum always swore blind that I saw Max Miller at the Finsbury Park but I don't remember it. And I think I'd have remembered Max Miller. In fact I think he'd be impossible to forget.

I decided there and then that I wanted to spend the rest of my life in theatres, and almost immediately they (whoever 'they' are) started pulling them down. And I did take it personally. Still do. Tearing down a variety theatre is like demolishing an operating theatre and telling the surgeon to do his heart transplants in a garage instead. With pissed nurses. Thank God performers don't matter, eh?

Of course I listened to the radio too (sorry, the 'wireless'), not just the music but the comedy shows like 'Take it From Here', 'Ray's a Laugh' and arguably the biggest of them all 'Educating Archie' with ventriloquist Peter Brough and his dummy Archie Andrews. (Yes, I know, but everyone's done the 'ventriloquist on the radio' bit before so I'll make no comment here). I had an Archie Andrews doll myself and toyed with ventriloquism for a while, then someone gave me a banjolele and I toyed with that. I didn't know how to tune it properly so I tuned it to an open major chord, an understanding I can only assume I got from primary school. I loved it, but I think I loved the 'drum' part of it most and eventually separated it from the neck and used it as… well, as a drum. There's no doubt that the combination of the theatre, radio (sorry, 'wireless') and TV sparked a passion for entertainment of some sort – unfocused, certainly, but I wanted to be in show business somehow. Then, when I was about eight, we moved from the hardware shop to a house in Hornsey. And that was where my troubles started.

The Evil Dead...

The house was a large one – seven rooms, kitchen, bathroom and cellar – and oddly laid out; two rooms on the ground floor, another on a slightly lower level at the back with the kitchen behind it, two rooms on the first floor, one room and bathroom on a kind of mezzanine level at the front and a small attic room at the top. The odd layout meant that the hall was high, sort of a floor and a half, and it had a mosaic floor and stained-glass door and surround. We effectively lived in four of these rooms – the lower back room was our family room, the front room was for guests, I slept in the first of the first-floor rooms, my parents' bedroom was on the mezzanine bit at the front, and in the attic room my dad had put a half-size billiard table. It had some mod cons, wasn't in particularly easy reach of shops and amenities, you get the picture. I hope.

The house felt wrong from the start. If I was in a room on my own I would always feel a strong presence there with me. I was forever looking over my shoulder, and when that revealed nothing I would look behind chairs, in cupboards, anywhere someone might be hiding. And there was always a skin-crawling sensation, really unsettling, and so powerful that I'm getting it now just writing about it. Hard to describe, but it felt like every hair on my body was tingling, on the alert, like a cat when it senses something threatening. These sensations were at their worst on the first floor, which had an atmosphere of pure dread about it, so much so that I would close my eyes and run down the stairs rather than encounter...what? That was the most unsettling thing of all –

what was causing all this? So far I'd seen nothing, heard nothing, but something was there all right. And one night it decided to make its presence felt.

My room was directly under the billiard room, and I had just gone to bed when I heard the unmistakeable sound of billiard balls being dropped on the floorboards above me. I froze, literally, ice cold and paralysed with fear. I waited for it to stop but it didn't, and the longer it went on, the greater was my need to go to my parents' room and tell them what was happening. That, though, would have meant me crossing the first-floor landing. Was that what it wanted? I took this for as long as I could bear it, then, unable to stand it any longer, I got out of bed. But as I was making for the door a cat screeched just outside my bedroom window. The noise startled me so much I got back into bed and the next thing I knew it was morning.

Of course I told my dad what had happened and he tried to explain it away by suggesting the sounds I'd heard had been a door banging in a draft. But I knew what I'd heard and I felt sure he knew it too. It never happened again, but the sensations of dread never disappeared and I have never been gladder to leave anywhere than I was to leave that house. Of course I shared all my anxieties with my mum and dad but they told me it was just my imagination. Bear in mind, I was only ten or eleven at the time; I knew nothing about ghosts, nothing about madness. All I knew was either the house was wrong or I was, and I didn't find out which until we moved.

It was while living in that house that I first became aware of the sound of the electric guitar. I was still playing records, of course, particularly Johnny Ray's 'Look Homeward Angel' which I played until you could hardly hear the music any more for the surface noise (old people will know what I mean) but the electric guitar came via the theme music to a TV show I enjoyed called 'Stranger than Fiction'. It was a catchy little tune and the sound sort of captivated me but I couldn't make out what instrument was doing the playing. I remember asking my dad but he didn't know either and it remained a mystery for years until I found out it was played by Bert Weedon and he was damping the strings. I knew nothing of such things which explains my confusion. Still, confused or not it sowed a seed that sprouted like a beanstalk and ain't stopped sprouting yet.

I'm a firm believer in the notion that the things that affect the rest of our lives usually start around that age. It's as if we suddenly get a flash of who we really are, and I got another one of those one day when I was reading a children's annual. I was leafing nonchalantly through the pages when I came across a half-page article, illustrated with a little blue and white drawing, explaining how families in some parts of the world would celebrate Christmas by going outside and playing together naked in the snow and something in my head exploded. Not literally, obviously, that would be ridiculous, but it's impossible to explain the effect that sentence had on me. It felt like an electric shock. In seven words it contradicted everything I'd ever been led to believe.

Naked? There's no such thing as 'naked', this is England! Naked? In the *snow*? They'd come and take you away surely...Naked?   With your *parents*? How...what...if... who...I was captivated instantly. Here was a world I had never even dreamed of, a freer world, a more exciting world and I could hardly contain myself. It was too rebellious to be true but there they were doing it, and if they were right we were *wrong*. That article kick-started an obsession I've never lost, and when I found out later that people actually broke the ice to swim I was so excited I could hardly breathe. Needless to say I didn't mention it to my parents 'cause I knew the reception it would get, but it was the most thrilling thing I'd ever heard of. Still is. And I've never met a single soul who agrees with me.

The final thing that happened during my occupancy of that house was that I passed the eleven-plus, which turned out to be the worst mistake I could possibly have made. I did it in all good faith (in both senses) as St Mary's told me it would win me a place at the Catholic Grammar School in nearby Tottenham - in theory a logical step. In practice, it traumatised me on the first day and kept me that way for five dreadful years.

Tone's browned off school days...

The moment I entered the school gates I was confronted by a scene I had never experienced before – large men pushing their faces into those of small children and screaming 'don't you be insolent, boy' with a venom that was quite alien to me. In similar vein we were herded into classrooms, where we learned of the punishment we could expect if we disobeyed orders or broke any of the rules – a strap made of rubber and stiffened with whalebone called a ferula (I looked it up in the dictionary once: it said 'Jesuit instrument of torture'). I had never experienced any kind of corporal punishment before and the idea terrified me.

It might have been a little more bearable if it had only been administered for serious offences as I was way too timid to commit any of those, but I soon found out it was used quite indiscriminately, often for nothing at all. Or nothing I could understand. Worse, it wasn't used on the spot – rather you were given a 'chit' with the number of strokes written on it and ordered to go at break time or after school, sometimes even the next day, to line up with any other miscreants for punishment. Alfred Hitchcock went to the same school (though not at the same time) and he said it was where he got the idea for suspense-filled horror movies. I'm not surprised.

My answer to all this was not just to keep my head down but to try to disappear altogether, to be as invisible as possible for as long as it took to get free of the place. This is not as easy as it sounds and it affects every aspect of your life – you can't spend all day trying to be invisible and then turn into

Bruce Forsyth when the bell goes, which is probably why I never had any friends or won any 'personality of the year' awards.

It didn't work anyway – I still had to do exams, recite Shakespeare and prove Pythagoras like everyone else, and being fat doesn't exactly help in the old invisibility stakes either. I also got thrashed like everyone else, though I still can't remember doing anything to deserve it. They say (or used to) that your schooldays are the happiest days of your life, but I can honestly say that however bad they've gotten since I always comfort myself with 'well, at least you're not at St Bastard's'.

As if being terrified of the regime wasn't enough I came to despise it as well. There seemed to be no justice or fairness and certainly no right of appeal, and while I barely understood the concept at the time I realised later it had delusions of being a public school, all 'prep', 'rugger' and 'tuck shops' and even, in the final year, a combined cadet force.

This was the final hammer-blow, being screamed at by an 'NCO' yelling 'you're not playing at soldiers, you *are* soldiers' when we were plainly nothing of the kind.

To make matters worse, if I looked fat and ugly in a school uniform I looked like something from the Goon Show in an army one, and to top it off I had to travel to and from school by bus. Now if you've ever tried to walk up or down the steel-edged stairs on a double-decker bus in army boots you'll know that every head turns in your direction to see

16

where the bloody racket is coming from, and that's not good if you're trying to remain invisible. The result was that I remained paranoid instead, convinced that every giggle I heard was one of mockery aimed at me.

There was an amusement arcade just up the road from school which boasted a BAL-AMi juke box, and I remember dropping in one afternoon and hearing Chuck Berry's 'School Days' which culminated with the line 'Hail, hail rock 'n' roll, deliver me from the days of old'. You can imagine how pertinent that was. I think I even believed it was possible then. After all, the kids we saw in American movies wore T-shirts and jeans and drove to school in hot rods, so it seemed possible. We went to school on the bus in blazers and caps (or worse) carrying satchels so I should have known better. How little I knew of old England, eh?

I begged my parents to get me out of St Bastard's and let me try out for the Italia Conte stage school (I'd read somewhere that one of my heroes, Anthony Newley, had gone there and I reckoned the 'Italia' part was sure to sway my mum) but it never happened. Instead I was obliged to endure five agonising years there and I left with just three O-levels, a nervous system like a shattered windscreen and all the self-assurance of a black soul singer at a Ku Klux Klan rally.

The Jesuits have a saying; 'give us the boy and we will give you back the man' and it certainly worked with me because it took me forty years to get over it, and only then with some serious help. It gave me PTSD, that school, with no parole and no compensation. What really infuriated me was that it did it in the name of Christianity. But, of course, so did the Spanish Inquisition.

Looking back on it now, I reckon the real irony of my years at St B's is that grammar schools were supposed to be for the elite, with the best teaching, the best careers advice and the best chance of going on to university, and I remember none of it. Compared with St Mary's the teaching struck me as fumbling, no one ever mentioned university and I never saw hide nor hair of a careers advisor.

The only thing I remember about careers was a piece of paper we were told to fill in, which included our names and classes and one question – proposed profession. I wrote 'musician' and never heard another word about university or careers. Presumably that one word was enough for them to disown me completely, but then it was enough for me to disown them too because I have never for a second considered being anything else. In fact simply being in an office or a factory has always made me feel almost terminally ill-at-ease, as if God was saying 'wrong, kid, not for you, get out of there fast'. This could once have been construed as an excuse for being bone idle (and often was) but a glance at my CV now shows I've been anything but. I just knew what I was, that's all.

You know, when things got tough, as they did pretty often, and Shirle hit me with the old 'well you wanted to be a musician' line I used to take the blame. Then one day I thought, wait a minute - no I didn't. Given the choice I'd rather like to be the CEO of some massive private corporation pulling down a few million a year, driving a Ferrari and wearing trousers that cost more than the average semi-detached house. I didn't *want* to be a musician, I *am* one and there's nothing I can do about it'. Well, same when I filled out that form at school.

Needless to say (but I will) we had sports at school but football wasn't one of them. Too common. Now I'm not saying I would have enjoyed football – I've no time for sport whatever its make and model - but I certainly didn't like 'rugger'. It was too much like mob violence for my liking and about the only time I tried to get the ball I broke my wrist, not the cheeriest thing for a guitar player to do. Luckily when I told the hospital doctor that I played guitar he organised some physiotherapy for me which not only helped the injury but kept me off school for an hour or two a week (or three or four if I walked slowly enough) thus turning a drama into a romance. (My left hand still doesn't quite fit right - it's never affected my guitar playing but it's a permanent momento of St Bastard's for which I am, obviously, eternally grateful). We had cricket at St B's, of course, but I didn't care for that either and it scared the hell out of me, especially after I copped a cricket ball full on the nut.

The one and only time I ever actually *tried* at any sport was one sports day when I was obliged to enter the 100yds race (oh, yards, remember them?) and decided that, since I had no chance of winning, I'd give it ruck all and see what happened. What happened was that after about 80yds I realised that I was in the lead and put the brakes on sharpish

– I didn't want to win anything for that bloody school and made sure I didn't. Looking back on it now the only sport I might have found useful, and I stress 'might', was boxing. I've never had a punch-up in my life, not even at school, and I reckon a bit of boxing might have given me some confidence, if only in being hit. But we didn't do boxing. Of course we didn't. I might have found it useful.

I said I've no time for any kind of sport. Well, just to keep you on your toes, I used to love ice hockey. Or, as it's known in the United States and Canada, 'hockey'. Harringay Arena was just around the corner from our old shops, which in turn (keep up) were just around the corner from the 'family' home, shared by the matriarch, Big Rena, and two of the brothers, Ernie and Bert, who later found enormous fame on Sesame Street. My aunt Vera and her husband, Les, lived nearby too, and it was they who started taking me to the Harringay Racers' home games.

Ice hockey is fast, and depends on great skill at two things – skating and stick control – and the pro players were fantastic at both. The Racers were captained for a while by a Canadian bloke called Bill Glennie, and I once saw him take a shot at goal from way out on the centre line. The light went on to signal that he'd scored, but it took the officials five minutes to find the puck. He'd hit it so hard it had embedded itself between the steel struts of the goal, and it took them another five minutes to dig it out. That's shooting, boy.

There weren't many teams in the British league back then – about six, I think –   and when they (whoever 'they' are) closed down Harringay Arena, Vera, Les and I started travelling to watch the Wembley Lions instead. You know that old line about lightning not striking twice in the same place? Well, in those days there were no Perspex shields around the rink, and one night a puck shot over the rail and hit a woman sitting near the front, knocking her out. She was taken away by St John Ambulance men, and I naturally hoped she was OK and was just wondering whether she would come back later when a puck shot over the rail and slammed straight into the back of the seat she'd been sitting in. Can you imagine how pissed off she'd have been if she'd said 'no, I'm fine, honestly. Anyway I'm bound to be safe now, I mean, you know what they say...'.

I loved ice hockey so much I actually thought for a while about taking it up professionally. I had a stick. And a puck. The only trouble was I used the stick as a 'guitar' and I never did learn to skate. I don't watch it on TV, partly because they don't show it and partly because it doesn't work on TV – it's too fast and the puck is too small. But then I don't watch any sport on TV unless it's Mohammed Ali, Roger Federer or Ronnie O'Sullivan.

Back in the day *everyone* watched Mohammed Ali's fights, and I do mean everyone. Even people who didn't like boxing or have a TV watched Ali, and I watched him because he was a genius and I love geniuses, which is why I watch O'Sullivan and Federer. Erratic at times, but when they're in the zone it's like watching a wizard doing impossible magic things. Like Hendrix.

Which reminds me, before I move on I must say one thing in favour of St Bastard's if only for the sake of balance. It introduced me to Mozart ('Howling Wolfgang') and Dvorak. More specifically, the 'Eine Kleine Nachtmusik' and the 'New World Symphony', two pieces of music I have never lost my passion for. I think I've owned the Mozart piece in just about every medium – 78, EP, LP, tape and CD – and of course once you 'find' Mozart he's got you forever. The downside of this is that I was only allowed to do music at school for the first two years. I can't remember why exactly, probably because they realised I liked it.

I can't end this bit without saying that I spent eleven years in total at two Catholic schools without ever once being sexually abused. Abused I was, certainly, at grammar school, but only physically, verbally and psychologically. Sexually, never. I must say this if only to refute the current assumption that everyone who went to a Catholic school must have been sexually abused by someone at some point. Of course I can't say *why* I wasn't sexually abused – maybe I just wasn't alluring enough. But I was surely vulnerable enough, and still I didn't get any action. I'm not trying to excuse the inexcusable, simply to point out it wasn't compulsory.

I spent two years going from the fire every day to the frying pan every night before we finally sold the frying pan. My mum and dad moved during the day when I was at school (yes, they gave me the address) and I arrived at tea time to find our new home was a flat above my dad's shop in Leyton, tiny compared to our old house but that wasn't my concern. This was where I would get my answer and I wanted it to be categorical, so I waited until the sun went down, then I went to the far corner of each room in turn and sat for a few minutes in the dark. Nothing. No skin-crawling, no invisible company, nothing. I wasn't crazy. (Actually the jury's still out on that but you know what I mean). Then, within days, my mum and dad both started talking about their own experiences in that house; unlike mine they were both visual.

My dad told me that his head had always frozen when he went up the stairs to the first floor, and one day when he looked up to the landing he saw the smoky figure of a man standing there. He would have stopped, he said, but my mum and I were following him and rather than frighten us he had kept walking. When he reached the top of the stairs, he said, the figure disappeared. My mum could top that. She had been going downstairs one night, she said, and when she looked down into the hall it was filled floor-to-ceiling with a massive shroud, arms outstretched and with a light emanating from around it. She didn't say so, but I reckon that must have been the catalyst for our move. I mean, wouldn't you?

Now you may be thinking 'don't be ridiculous, there's no such thing as ghosts'. If so, all I can say is 'bollocks'. I realise that some people have to experience things before they can accept or understand them, but if you honestly think I'm making it all up you might as well stop reading now. Because you're not going to believe a word I say from here on in anyway.

NB: You know you're supposed to remember what you were doing when you heard that Kennedy had been assassinated?

No? You're too young, obviously. Well, I remember where I was when I learned of the death of Buddy Holly, Richie Valens and the Big Bopper: I was standing on the landing of the flat above my dad's shop in Leyton staring at the headline in the Daily Mirror. I'd never had anyone die on me up to that point and I was devastated. It didn't seem real. I've felt the same about every other deceased musician I've heard about since. It always feels personal in a way I can't explain.

All Shook Up

Make no mistake about it, if Elvis Presley was the American messiah, Lonnie Donegan was ours. And we needed ours more. Like Elvis, Lonnie seemed to spring from nowhere, and fully armed. Lonnie paralleled Elvis in a number of uncanny ways – same source inspirations, same band line-up, same fresh approach – but where Elvis was a product of his environment and culture, Lonnie invented himself from scratch. Here, in very infertile soil. And having done it he soon perfected it with a vocal style and ability no one else came close to. There are thousands of Elvis impersonators; there has never been a single Lonnie impersonator because it's fucking impossible.

Lonnie called his music 'skiffle' but it was way more than that. Based on black and white American folk music – blues and country if you like – he reimagined it, re-wrote it and rearranged it, then sang and played it with a ferocious jazz understanding (honed through years playing with the likes of Ken Colyer and Chris Barber), backed up by a hand-picked trio of likely jazz musicians. He had a vocal range you couldn't buy in a shop, and he did something I've never heard any other singer do – he improvised more and more as a song went on, thus increasing the excitement levels verse after verse simply by the way he sang. Unique it was. Is.

We, at the time, were ten or eleven years old with no instruments and little money to buy them, while Lonnie was a seasoned pro with a band of top jazz musicians around him. We were like kids with catapults stalking a crack SAS squad.

We sung his songs and formed skiffle groups, thousands of them, but they were all crap and using crap, even home-made, instruments while he had the best of everything. But with his training we learned fast. The Shadows and the Beatles both started as skiffle groups and look what happened to them.

NB: The most fascinating thing about Lonnie, the Shadows and the Beatles is that despite having the same line-ups (two guitars, bass and drums) and being hot on each other's heels time-wise they couldn't have been more different if they'd tried (which, of course, they did). Their material was entirely different, their approaches were entirely different, their sounds were entirely different and each of them made brand new, unique, never-heard-anything-like-it-before music.

More, each of them was not only the best of its kind in England *by light years*, they were better than anything else *on earth*. There was nothing resembling Lonnie, even in America. There was no four-piece instrumental group as good as the Shadows, even in America. And the Beatles we all know about.

This had never happened in England before (we never produced an Ellington, an Armstrong or a Goodman) and, for my money, hasn't happened since. Since then it's been largely a matter of opinion, but no one at the time would have argued the point because the truth was obvious, and it was their records we all waited for, devoured and attempted to emulate.

NB: Swift thoughtette which I shall probably return to later – if Lonnie, the Shadows and the Beatles were two guitars, bass and drum bands fifty years ago, why does almost every band still consist of two guitars, bass and drums? Comedians don't still wear evening suits and tell mother-in-law jokes, we don't still light the streets with gas, it's fifty years later, chaps, why are you still…well you get the picture. Whatever happened to originality? Or am I being too original?

Back to the plot – sensing my interest my mum and dad bought me a guitar (of sorts), I bought a chord book and started to learn to accompany myself like Lonnie, but once I started I found the guitar taking over. Listening to the improvisations of Lonnie's sensational lead players (Jimmy Curry, Denny Wright and, finally, Les Bennetts) opened up a whole new world of possibilities and that became my aim. I wanted to be a guitar player. So blame them.

As I pointed out before my listening didn't start with Lonnie. I literally played those 78s until I wore 'em out, I listened to the radio (sorry, the 'wireless') and the wireless in those days played every conceivable kind of music at one time or another – 'Music While You Work', the 'Billy Cotton Band Show', 'Housewives' Choice', 'Family Favourites', even 'Children's Favourites' all featured a vast range of stuff from 'Nellie the Elephant' to 'The Dam Busters' March' and I ear'oled all of it.

And of course, people sang together in those days too, around the piano in the pub, round the piano in the front room at parties, even if no one could play the piano everyone gathered round it, and every household had a piano. Most people had a little specialist solo piece (always the same one) to delight the assembled masses with, and there was a pool of songs everybody seemed to know the words to (or some of the words) even though some of those songs were from a different generation. This sort of behaviour is quite inconceivable now. Have you seen the price of pianos?

Pre rock 'n' roll, popular music had a diversity and sophistication way in advance of almost anything since, and although I didn't realise it at the time it was all sinking in. If anything explains the diversity and sophistication of Lonnie, the Shadows and the Beatles, that's it. They were my age (or older) and grew up hearing the same things. I know guitar players, good ones, who grew up listening to rock music and they don't have a fraction of that understanding or facility. It also explains the speed of our development, from a standing start in 1957 to Sgt. Pepper ten years later. It doesn't seem possible now.

The 1950s really were the best times for music. No, it's not up for discussion - historically speaking, never in the field of human conflict have so many been exposed to so much by so many, all of it different and some of it brand spanking new. Stravinsky and Sinatra were on the wireless, but so was 'The Billy Cotton Band Show' and 'Music While You Work'. We were awash with orchestral 'light music', much of it by Eric Coates and much of it brilliant, we had jazz – modern from Miles and Dave Brubeck, 'trad' from Kenny Ball and Acker Bilk – we had novelty records, musical interludes in comedy programmes, we had skiffle, we had rock 'n' roll, we had rhythm & blues, we had 'My Fair Lady' and the never-equalled 'West Side Story'... shit, brother, the one thing you never heard anyone say was 'I don't know, there's just not enough *variety* is there?'

NB: Should any of this get in the charts it was classed as 'pop' music, short for 'popular' because a lot of people bought it. Meaning it was popular. That was what 'pop' meant. Only later did someone decide that 'pop music' was a type of music regardless of whether it was popular or not, and that if something that wasn't 'pop music' was popular enough to get in the charts it still didn't count as 'pop music' because it wasn't. These days nothing that isn't 'pop music' gets in the charts anyway, so problem solved. Or exacerbated, I'm not sure.

I adored rock 'n' roll when it came along. Of course I did, we all did. It took over the world, and politicians of all denominations must be kicking themselves that they didn't think of it. The first rock 'n' roll records I got were 'That'll be the Day' by the Crickets and 'Rip It Up' by Bill Haley and the Comets, and I followed those up with as many Elvis, Little Richard, Duane Eddy, Jerry Lee Lewis, Everly Brothers, Lloyd Price, Ricky Nelson, Coasters, Neil Sedaka and Connie Francis records as my pocket money would allow. I bought Lonnie too, of course, and the Shadows, and just about anything else that took my fancy, and I knew the charts by heart.

I've thought about this a lot since then, and I *think* one of the things that propelled our own learning at such a rate was that we, like our parents and grandparents, bought 'singles' with just one track per side, firstly on 78s and then on 45s, because when you only buy two tracks you tend to listen to them over and over again for days at a time and, hence, end up knowing every tiny detail of them. When albums came along I noted the tendency to play a whole side without stopping, then CDs allowed you to play the whole album without stopping, and the rise of the internet and the iPod meant effectively an endless stream of music, none of which you listen to in any detail at all. I could be wrong. I'm not, but I could be.

NB: Some of the greatest pop records of that era were only a minute and a half long, some not even that. Fabulous! Get in, make your statement and get out again, fabulous. It meant you got more records per hour on the radio (sorry, 'wireless'), if you didn't like a record it would be over pretty quickly, and if you did like one you bought it and played it as many times as you liked. Fabulous.

Well, a few years ago I heard Dale Winton (sorry about that, I was in the car) play a record on the radio and announce afterwards 'great record but terrible value at only two minutes ten seconds' so for what it's worth I'll say it again: 1, if it's on the radio it's *free*. And 2, if you like it you can buy it once and play it over and over again, non-stop, for the rest of your life. What 'terrible value'?

Anyway, I would buy whichever record I fancied at the time, put it on and play along with it until I sounded as if I was actually on the record myself. This I did over and over again with record after record until I could pretty well play along with, and adapt to, almost anything instantly. I did almost all of this by ear, as did most of my fellow autodidacts, so by the time Cliff Richard's 'Move it!' came along in 1958 I was ready for it. But first came a diversion. Or expansion. Probably both.

I was advised to try out for a skiffle group that had been formed by some people at my local church, and I went along to the church hall to discover it wasn't a skiffle group at all but a little dance band – no guitars, just trumpet, trombone, saxes and piano. This was my first experience of what English people knew about music. Fuck all. Anyway, they put a piece of music in front of me - I can see it now, 'The Way You Look Tonight' arranged by Jimmy Lally – and it was in Eb. My chord knowledge at the time encompassed the usual skiffle and rock 'n' roll keys (E, A, G, D and C) but I was bright enough to know that Eb was a semitone below E so I played an E chord one fret down and there I was.

They started playing 'The Way You Look Tonight' arranged by Jimmy Lally in Eb and I think I managed to play three or four chords before it finished, which must have been good enough because I was invited to join the band (thus disproving the old adage that a flatter E will get you nowhere) and before long I was playing 'The Way You Look Tonight', 'Cheek to Cheek' and 'American Patrol' in all sorts of keys. Great training. But, more importantly, this lot (all college types and quite a lot older than me) introduced me to jazz. More of that later.

While I was now free of the house of terror I was still obliged to serve my sentence at the school that compassion forgot every day, but you can't win them all. Well, I couldn't. And that wasn't the only thing I couldn't win. The stars of the day – Lonnie, Elvis, Cliff etc – were all lithe good-looking men with fabulous Pompadour haircuts; I was short, fat and ugly and my hair just wouldn't. Some of the kids at school were no better looking than me, of course, but some of them were handsome with great hair too, as were plenty out and about in the street, and like any adolescent I was mortified. We all want to look like our idols, right? And the Buddha wasn't my idol.

If I'd had any self-confidence I might have been able to ride out these problems, but school had ensured I had none of that. Low self-esteem doesn't even begin to cover it. I dreamed of having low self-esteem. For a while I tried to cover this up by becoming Tony Hancock, doing my best to assume his lugubrious persona on the grounds, I think, that I could at least get some laughs that way. He did. And he was *popular*, so popular that he emptied the pubs when he was on TV. I, unfortunately, was more likely to empty a pub by being in the pub and eventually I gave up on Hancock. Years later so did he, but that's another story.

NB: In the 1980s, having bought and read Bertrand Russell's 'History of Western Philosophy', I discovered that Hancock took a copy of the same book with him everywhere he went. Hancock's Christian names were Anthony John, too. Coincidence? Certainly.

My weight I was powerless to understand let alone deal with. In the 'real' world it didn't seem to matter much – it hadn't held back Fats Waller and it wasn't holding back Fats Domino – but when you're an adolescent you might as well look like John Merrick as be fat. (I later realised, because it became too obvious to miss, that I pile on weight whenever I'm in a stressful situation I can't see a way out of. You know that logo Billy Connolly has on the back of his jacket, 'Too Old to Die Young'? If I'd thought of it earlier I could have had 'Fat When Cornered' on mine. It's not as good as Billy's but it's accurate). My hair I tried to correct with lacquer, creams, multiple trips to the barber's, blow-drying, even hair nets, but I might have well have asked it to play the cello for all the co-operation I got.

NB: Talking of Billy Connolly, he reckons that everyone at some time in their life has peered into the mirror and gone 'Yeah, looking good!' Billy's wrong.

To make matters worse, this was about the time I started noticing girls. We had none at school, of course, that would have been far too reasonable, but there was one who lived across the road from us who was a real darling. It was even her name – Linda Darling – and she mesmerised me. Recognising this, my mum suggested my mate Dave and I invite her and her friend to tea, which was one of the worst ideas my mum ever had as Linda and her friend spent the whole time giggling at Dave and ignoring me completely. Yes, I know, get the violins out, but at the time it was so humiliating I would have wished I was dead if I'd thought Linda and her friend would have noticed.

Now of course this was the fifties, which meant kids my age knew nothing about sex. And I mean nothing. At all. We didn't even giggle about it behind the bike sheds at school, partly because we didn't have any bike sheds but mainly because we didn't know what it was. I had known for years that riding the arm of a chair produced intriguingly pleasant sensations, a bit like scratching an itch, which prepared me for subsequent years of self-abuse, but I had no real idea what I was abusing myself about.

I realise this is a controversial thing to say, but I envy 'young people' now who have pornography on tap on the internet because at least they're not living in ignorance. I'm not talking children here obviously (at least I hope it's obvious) but once the hormones start kicking in a little knowledge is a valuable thing, much more valuable than an embarrassed information blackout. I know some people want it banned because it might warp 'young people's minds' but what warps a young person's mind quicker than telling them that their natural feelings are dirty or perverted? As for sixteen-year-olds, once they're legally entitled to 'do it' it's ridiculous to say they shouldn't watch anyone else doing it. It's like passing your driving test and having the examiner say 'Congratulations, now don't let me catch you watching anyone else drive'.

NB: You may be thinking 'you don't need pornography to give young people information, they get sex lessons at school'. OK, but let's be honest – any teacher who tried to teach sex properly at school would either be sacked, arrested or both, because sex ain't like maths or IT, and that's especially true of the oral exams. You can teach maths and IT without ever having to suggest they might be enjoyable – do that with sex and you ain't teaching it properly. Correct? Correct. Thank you.

Back to the world of dreams - in my day sex wasn't even mentioned, much less displayed in all its aspects in full colour. In fact the first naked woman I ever saw was in black and white, in a Health & Efficiency magazine someone brought to school. She wasn't posing provocatively, just standing like a statue, but it was some sort of information at least. (Actually this is somewhat disingenuous, as the first naked woman I ever saw was my aunt Vera. I was about six at the time and I walked in on her just as she got out of the bath. It didn't last long – in, scream, out again, half a second max – but it's still imprinted on my mind. Weird, eh?).

Of course by the time I was approaching parole from St Bastard's I'd caught the odd furtive glimpse of the only available glamour mag, Playboy, which sent my libido into overdrive, but Playboy was classy with no full-frontals so I still had no idea of what went on 'twixt a lady's lower extremities, nor would I have for a few years yet. Still, it gave me a lifelong appreciation of tits for which I am eternally grateful. I still think tits are the most wonderful things on earth, and I refuse to apologise for it. Not only are they beautiful and sexy, they're like fingerprints – no two (pairs) the same. Fabulous. Thank you, God.

NB: This observation does not hold true in the case of surgically-enhanced knockers, which I regard as an offence

35

against all things good and holy, especially me. Have you seen 'em? I mean, they're supposed to move, for God's sake – the enhanced ones look as if someone has shoved a couple of bowling balls in there. Horrible, they are. And expensive too. Leave 'em alone and buy a nicer car or something, take a trip, anything. You know it makes sense.

Needless to say there were no tits for Tone. No lips, arms, feet or anything else, for that matter. So I ploughed all my attention into music, which was no hardship as I adored everything about it – listening to it, reading about it, trying to play it, everything. Of course it was exciting in those days, really exciting. Rock 'n' roll was new, electric guitars and amps were new, and for a few brief months the TV had 'Oh Boy!' on Saturday evenings, and that was sensational. I usually went to go to my aunt Vera's (yes, that one) for tea on Saturdays and watched it there.

Created by Jack Good, it was fast and furious and featured most of our top stars and the occasional visiting American. It also boasted a sensational 'house band' in the shape of Lord Rockinham's XI, a saxes and guitars powerhouse led by Harry Robinson that backed up every act on the show and did it brilliantly. They had a female organist too (Cherry Wainer) and went on to have a couple of hit records of their own. Fab. (Incidentally, despite the very rock 'n roll nature of their name, I believe the original Lord Rockingham's XI was actually a cricket team! Clever bit of pilfering, that one).

I can't remember now whether Joe Brown was the resident lead guitarist on that show or its follow-up 'Boy Meets Girl' but I can remember how important he was to me. He *bent strings*, for God's sake, and he had a beautiful guitar (Gibson 335 if you're interested) and I stole stuff from him wholesale. Not the guitar, obviously, he swapped that for a Les Paul (which he hated) and Roy Wood now owns it. Joe has tried to buy it back from him but Roy won't sell it, bastard.

And on top of all that was the jazz I mentioned earlier. The Royal Blues took me to see the Count Basie Orchestra, the Dizzie Gillespie Quintet, the John Coltrane Quintet (with Eric Dolphy) as well as a number of BBC Jazz Club recordings and a few Sunday nights at the Marquee with the Johnny Dankworth Big Band and the Dudley Moore Trio.

Coltrane's band intrigued me more than words can say. To my ears it sounded like five kids who had found instruments in a garage and just started blowing and bashing them – chaos. But it was powerful, passionate chaos, and when the unison passages emerged they were as tight as a duck's arse. These blokes knew what they were doing even if I didn't, and the only thing that seemed to be keeping regular time was the drummer's high-hat. So fascinated was I by this that when I got home I practised for hours keeping time with my high-hat (yes, I played drums too) while playing nonsense on the rest of the kit. It was the only way I knew to replicate what I'd heard.

The Count Basie band was far easier to understand and downright fabulous to listen to, but I was mystified when I spotted guitarist Freddie Green playing a different chord every two beats in a 12-bar blues. I was pretty sure there were only three chords in a 12-bar blues (well, three-ish) but he obviously had other ideas about which I was clueless. He also played an acoustic guitar, yet in the quieter passages you could hear it quite clearly. Fascinating.

Dudley Moore was a phenomenal jazz pianist, a fact that got rather overshadowed later by his other impressive gifts. He not only had the ears, the chops and the imagination of a great jazz musician, but his playing was full of fun, too, and he had an uncanny empathy and rapport with his drummer, Chris Karen, which meant they would spend whole sets grinning at each other and phrasing together quite spontaneously. And the Dankworth band, unusually, featured a tuba in the line-up (Ron Snyder, I think) which gave it a unique sound.

I saw the legendary drummer Phil Seaman sit in with the Dankworth band, and a young Jack Bruce, too, on double bass, and I learned a valuable lesson one night when Dankworth and his lead alto player, Roy East, shared fours, because Dankworth played twenty notes to every one of East's and both approaches worked equally well. Unfortunately I learned this lesson in theory only, because for most of my life I always overplayed everything.

Those gigs were like paradise, all of them. I didn't understand all the music, but the musicians playing it obviously did and my ears were getting an Olympic-style workout. I can't say the same for the Royal Blue gigs as they probably sounded bloody awful. I was playing drums with the band by then, but insisted on getting my guitar out and forming a rock 'n' roll band within it as a kind of mid-gig extra.

Unfortunately, though my playing was coming on I really wasn't up to singing the hits of the day like 'Handy Man' by Jimmy Jones or Del Shannon's 'Runaway' so that band (Stapp Berry and the Bachelors, named from western hero Wyatt Berry Stapp Earp) probably sounded bloody awful too, and bloody awful with a fat unattractive singer to boot. God, I make it sound romantic, don't I?

I've been asked if I remember anything amusing about those early gigs but the truth is I have a very selective memory and it has selected to remember hardly anything. I remember that Joan Cunningham, one of our saxes, went on to work with the much-respected Ivy Benson Band. I remember we once left our amps on a village green after a gig – a bloke walking to work the next morning noticed some 'gravestones' that hadn't been there the day before, went to investigate and we got our amps back. But apart from that, nothing. How can that be, I hear you cry? Me too.

It was while I was with the Royal Blue Dance Band that I got arrested. It came about when one of the band, who worked at Ilford Films in… well, Ilford… invited us all to go along with him to a firm's 'do'. None of the band drank, or if they did not above a couple of halves, and having enjoyed a convivial evening we were on our way back to the car when we were grabbed by two coppers, marched down to Ilford nick and charged by a sour-faced sergeant with something like 'behaviour likely to cause a breach of the peace'. As far as I knew we hadn't done any 'behaviour' of any kind, though we might have been laughing. Perhaps that was it.

Either way, it so happened that one of the band's sister worked for a very successful and high-profile lawyer named Fellows (he'd recently defended in something known as the Ranchhouse Murders in Essex) and she asked him if he wouldn't mind defending us. He laughed when she asked him, she said, but agreed to do it for her. So, on the day of our trial we were waiting in the corridor outside the court when the desk sergeant from Ilford nick approached us with a smug grin on his face and asked who was defending us. When we told him you could have heard the sound of his chin hitting the floor from Watford. He stormed off, and when our case was called we stood in the dock and heard the two coppers who had arrested us swear under oath that we had forced an elderly couple into the road, which was very big news indeed to us as the street had been deserted at the time.

Fellows asked them, one by one, if the elderly couple were in court. No, they said. 'But as material witnesses you do have their names and addresses?' said Fellows. No, they said, and the magistrate threw the case out of court. Now the point of this story, as far as I was concerned, was this – if two coppers were prepared to lie under oath to get a conviction on a naff little charge like 'behaviour likely to cause a breach of the peace' what the hell would they do in a murder case? And that, m'lud, is the evidence for the disenchanted.

So for a couple of years it was the hell of school followed by hours in my room with records and a guitar, interspersed with the odd (probably very odd) gig and nocturnal ruminations about women. But there was one other bright spot in my life and for a few short weeks it shone like a beacon. It was a TV series called 'The Strange World of Gurney Slade' starring Anthony Newly and it transfixed me in a way nothing else on the box did. It certainly didn't empty the pubs like Hancock, in fact its reception was so lukewarm it got moved to a later timeslot and ran for six episodes only but it made a huge impression on me because, I think, its lead character was an isolated loner with off-the-wall ideas and observations and I recognised a kindred spirit.

So when I read that Newley had written a musical with Leslie Bricusse and was starring in it in the West End I coerced my dad into taking me and thus I got to see 'Stop the World I Want to Get Off', probably the most ground-breaking musical of its time. 'Impressed' would be an understatement and I remained a huge fan of Anthony Newley until he went to America and sort of disappeared into the Las Vegas lounges. I still think he was one of the most important performers of his day and I can't believe he's not better recognised for it.

Incidentally I Googled 'Gurney Slade' recently just to see if there was any mention of it at all and to my delight I spotted a site advertising the whole series for sale on DVD. As is well known, TV companies in those days used to wipe video tapes as soon as they'd been used and I had always assumed that was the fate of 'Gurney Slade' but it turns out 'Gurney

Slade' wasn't done on video but on film. It's in black and white, but it's perfect and I recommend it.

I must have discovered Django Reinhardt by then, too, because I've got photos that prove it, and I can't begin to tell you what a revelation that was. Well I can 'cause I just have, but I mean… I actually remember thinking 'you can do *that* with a guitar?' It was hard to believe then, and frankly it's still hard to believe now. It's like he was saying 'come and have a go if you're talented enough' and I wasn't. Few of us are.

Ah, yes, of course, I've just remembered where I got those Django records. I had left school by then (though 'left school' hardly conveys the feeling – it felt more like I'd been liberated by the Russian army) and got my first job in an insurance office in the City of London. It was as dull as it sounds, but I learned to use the Tube on my own and there were two likely girls in the office who, I think, regarded me as a pet. Not as in 'Penthouse Pet', obviously, more like a stray they'd adopted, but at least it wasn't hostile.

More importantly in those days, before Thatcher raised property prices so that only the Sultan of Brunei could afford them, the City of London was home to little record stalls, mostly up back alleys, and it was there that I availed myself of albums by Wes Montgomery, Barney Kessell, Miles Davis, Duke Ellington and Muggsy Spanier, albums that changed my life.

Wes was a gob-smacking revelation. The first track up on his 1960 album 'The Incredible Jazz Guitar of Wes Montgomery'

('Airegin') features a solo so overwhelmingly brilliant I still don't understand where it comes from. Spanier was a white Chicago cornet player, and his record 'The Great 16' (a compilation of tracks recorded by his Ragtime Band six years before I was born) taught me the blues, while Miles represented a beauty I'd never quite heard before. The first track up on his album 'Working with the Miles Davis Quintet' ('It Never Entered My Mind') remains one of the most beautiful things I ever heard. I couldn't understand note one of any of this music, but I adored it all.

NB: You will note from this that I never just bought records from my own era or of one particular style, and I've never understood people who do. This country seems to be full of 'rock' fans or 'indie' fans or, even worse, fans of 'eighties' music or 'nineties' music.

You hear it on quiz shows all the time – 'what kind of music do you like'? 'Oh, eighties music'. I always want to say '*what* eighties music? Eighties jazz? Eighties reggae? Eighties' *violin concertos*'? 'Eighties' is not a style of music, it's a fucking chronological period you knob. Well, I bought anything and everything, some of it new and some of it, like Spanier, Ellington and Mozart, older than I was. If it was good it didn't matter. Still doesn't. Great art doesn't date.

This, of course, was a time when Shadows ruled the earth, all red Strats, Precision basses and Vox AC30s. God how we envied them, all us would-be musicians, for their gear, their poise, their sound, their records. They were cool with four capital Cs and a few Os and we all learned to play 'Apache'.

43

Not as well as Hank – no one's ever played it as well as Hank – but I could play it at least, which was more than I could do with Wes or Miles. So when my parents moved to Essex and I found myself a member of the Vibratones it was Shadows stuff we played.

Not a bad little band, the Vibratones, though not as good at the Shadows stuff as the Nightriders, another Essex band, whose dads had good enough jobs to provide them with the same Fender/Vox/Gretsch drum kit kit as the Shadows used themselves. Flash bastards. They had learned the Shadows' stuff note for note, mistakes as well, and did all the steps too. We were a little more varied in our approach, and when the Beatles came along we went along for the ride. Which the Nightriders couldn't do with their Strats. Perhaps they part-exed them.

Feeling that 'Vibratones' was a tad old fashioned we tried to come up with a new name for the band around this time, and if you've ever done this yourself you'll know how tricky it can be. I searched the titles in my record collection looking for inspiration and came across 'I'm Just a Rolling Stone' but I discarded it straight away. 'The Rolling Stones'? God no, that sounds *awful*. We eventually picked the name 'VIPs'.

You know, we talk now about technological innovation but Leo Fender and Dick Denney innovated technologically way ahead of their time(s) and got it right first time, so right their innovations haven't been bettered sixty years later. How fab is that?

Fender's Telecaster, the first solid electric guitar, was designed from scratch in 1948 and is still being produced because it still works. We didn't get them here because there was a wartime trade embargo still in place, but we saw them in photos and heard them on records. The Precision bass came along in 1952 and the Stratocaster two years later. We didn't get those either for the same reason, but I saw a Strat in 1958 when Buddy Holly did TV's 'Sunday Night at the London Palladium' and I couldn't believe it.

If Leo's offspring were unavailable here, Dick Denney's Vox AC 15 was designed and made here, and while we couldn't have afforded any of them they were the wonders of the age. Then Cliff sent to America for a Strat, and by 1960 the trade embargo had gone and the Shadows were replete with Fenders and Vox AC30s. So what, you may ask. Well…

Nothing sounded as good as Fenders and Vox AC30s, which meant that we couldn't sound as good as anyone who had them. More to the point, nothing still sounds as good as a Fender or a Vox, which is why most people (who can afford them) still use them. New guitar and amp designs have come and gone in droves since then, but watch the telly and you'll see. What else can you say that about? Are you still driving a Ford Popular or playing 78s on a wind-up gramophone? Oh, well you're very unusual then.

Like everyone else I was in love with Stratocasters in those days, obsessed even. Since then I've played loads and owned three, and a Strat was my main guitar for many years. But they found their way out of my life because I don't play that way. Bizarrely, though, even though I don't want one any more I'm still in love with the *idea* of Strats. I sort of *dream* them perfect for me even though I know they're not. I guess dreams are impossible to kill, and I'm delighted about it. Reality's only a pain in the arse anyway.

You know, if you're younger than me (and who isn't) it's impossible to understand the level of excitement generated back then by Fenders and Voxes. It was like they'd come from Vulcan, a sort of close encounter of the 'wow' kind, and being 'close' was enough to cause serious salivating.

I remember Andy Daniels turning up at school one day, jumping up and down because he'd seen a bloke with a guitar case the night before, asked what it was and been shown a real live Precision bass. Mickey Gower, another bassist, told me he'd danced all the way home from the West End to the East End because he'd seen a Strat in the window of Selmer's in Charring Cross Road, and the Tremelos' Alan Blakley told me that when the Trems first got their Vox/ Fender gear they'd set it up with the guitars hanging over the amps and watched as the audience came in and stared at it. 'The gear was our support act' he said. When did any kind of 'technology' do *that*?

Voxes and Fenders apart, it's hard to appreciate how primitive musical equipment was in the late 50s and early 60s, a situation made worse by being skint and ignorant. Most of the guitars were either unplayable or fell apart PDQ, and the amps we could afford were lashed up, as often as not, and tiny by today's standards – 15 watts if you were lucky. In fact a lot of people thought you plugged an electric guitar straight into the mains socket, can you imagine that? Some even did. Only once, but they did. There were no guitar leads as such – we made our own – and string gauges were unheard of. But what we lacked in money and finesse we somehow made up for with inventiveness.

My pièce de résistance came about through lack of an echo unit to recreate the repeat sounds on the end of the Shadows' 'Kon Tiki'. Ready? You're not going to believe this but… I split the screen wire on my guitar lead and fixed each end to a Bulldog clip, so that when the clip was tight the connection was made. Then, by treading on the clip and opening it I could break the connection, thus recreating the echo sound at the end of 'Kon Tiki'. Brilliant, eh? Or mental, depending on which way you look at it. Courtesy of my dad, I later acquired a proper Watkins Copycat, which meant I could do the echo effect on the strings at the end of Carol King's 'It Might As Well Rain Until September' too. Class!

I learned to drive in Essex, and I got my second day-job in the tiny site office of an asphalt roofing company near Southend run by two very nice blokes called Norman and Bert. Bert was often out with one of the gangs (roofing, not bank-robbing) so there was usually only two of us in the office and sometimes only me, which suited me fine, and although I had to work on Saturday mornings I didn't mind because there wasn't much to do and it meant I could listen to 'Saturday Club' on the radio, the only pop show on the BBC and two hours of bliss. (The term 'pop' could be a trifle misleading here, because Saturday Club played all sorts of records and had 'live' performances by all manner of different 'pop' acts like Adam Faith, Shane Fenton & the Fentones and the Beatles, trad jazz from Kenny Ball, Acker Bilk or Terry Lightfoot, country music from the Lorne Gibson Trio and just about anything else that was vaguely current. Its presenter, Brian Matthew, is still presenting 'Sounds of the Sixties' at the time of writing).

Having learned to drive I drove, to work and to gigs, in my old man's Commer Cob, which I expertly fitted out with a radio, i.e. I bought a radio, bolted it to the parcel shelf and wedged a speaker on top. That van had the best gearbox I've ever encountered, and the radio allowed me to listen to Radio Luxembourg ('fabulous 208') on my way back from gigs, which was more important than it sounds. Luxembourg only broadcast in the evenings and faded in and out like it was coming from Mars, but it played pop records, hard core, non-stop until about midnight, and some of them were classics.

The one that made the biggest impact on me, though, was probably Johnny Tillotson's 'Poetry in Motion', and more because of the backing than John's vocals. The session band and singers were so together it captivated me, especially the way they phrased the middle eight. There must have been at least eight in the band and half-a-dozen singers, but they were so tight they sounded like one man and that, I decided, was the bench mark. I wanted to get good enough to play with people who could do that, and once I'd spotted it I started noticing it on other records I had.

48

It didn't click then, but I later realised they were all American. That level of tightness comes from a natural feel that English musicians generally don't have, and it's that feel I look for instinctively in everything I hear. For me it's the wheels on the car, and however flash the paintwork or supercharged the engine; if the car ain't got no wheels, it ain't going nowhere. There's a ton of flash, supercharged music some people go crazy for that leaves me cold and that's why. No wheels.

My big 'pop' guitar heroes back then were probably James Burton, who played on most of Ricky Nelson's records, and the bloke who played on Connie Francis' best tracks and executed the finest guitar solo on any pop record, the one in 'Lipstick on Your Collar'. I only found out recently that this was jazz guitarist George Barnes, which makes perfect sense. I was never one to copy solos note-for-note, but I made an exception with Burton's solo on 'It's Late' because it was short, bendy and *fabulous,* and Buddy Holly's solo on 'Peggy Sue Got Married' because it was melodic and sounded great. I didn't even try to play the 'Lipstick' solo – I know when I'm beaten.

I saw some extremely informative gigs in the local clubs around this time, including Screaming Lord Sutch and Georgie Fame & the Blue Flames, and the Vibratones did a couple of reasonable support gigs including one at Greenwich Town Hall with Vince Eager. I remember it particularly because the audience were so friendly that by the end of the night we'd had a chat with both of them. Naturally, once the Beatles had taken over we all wanted to be Scousers and play at the Cavern, but we weren't and we couldn't so we didn't.

I did get my first publishing contract, though, and three records were released with my name on the writing credits, quite a big deal for someone from a little Essex band. I made my recording debut with the Vibratones (a demo of 'Honey Don't' and the instrumental 'Night Train') in the studio of Pepe Rush, the man who built the first bass amp in England, and our bass player, Dave Valentine, introduced me to the music of Chet Atkins, so it wasn't all bad. In truth all I wanted to be was pro. It ate at me day and night. I even auditioned for a couple of pro bands – the aforementioned Screaming Lord Sutch, and a trad band I can't remember the name of for whom I auditioned on drums. They're the only two auditions I ever failed.

NB: My good friend and great bass player Tony Bell once auditioned for David Sutch too, but he actually got the job. Thrilled, he bought a brand new Precision bass and was happily playing away on his first gig when 'this apparition appeared before me, ripped the bass off my shoulders, threw it to the ground and stamped it to pieces'. Tone was left, he said, picking up bits of bass from the stage, or the bits he could see through the tears anyway. He said His Lordship apologised afterwards and bought him a new bass, but that was David Sutch for you. Off stage he was as quiet and unassuming as you could get, but his act was no showbiz pretence. He really was nuts. Great, though, and he always had a great band too. Sadly missed.

Having mentioned the enormous variety of music around when I was growing up, it still amazes me how jazz was accepted as part of the furniture back then. These days it's treated like some sort of mental illness or secret vice, but I well remember that the biggest local venue in Westcliffe in the early '60s featured us rock 'n' roll types three or four nights a week and the Southend Modern Jazz Quintet (SMJQ) every Wednesday, with no noticeable drop-off in customers. They were bloody good, mind you, but can you imagine the moaning it would engender now? 'Fucking jazz? What d'you want to put that shit on for'?

As for my love life, I was seventeen by then and I hadn't had as much as a smile from a bird much less a kiss or a fondle. Denny Laine once told me that one of his prime motivations for taking up the guitar had been that it doubled his chances of pulling. I actually played the guitar, and pretty well too, and women still stayed away from me in droves. If I hadn't played the guitar they'd probably have stoned me.

Before I end this trip back into the '50s and early '60s I must mention the situation regarding drink and drugs. We didn't have any. We heard rumours that modern jazz musicians smoked something called 'reefers' but nothing passed our lips more exotic than Senior Service, and pills were things doctors gave you when you were ill.

Booze was around, of course, but not usually where we were – it's a sobering thought now (see what I did there?) that the two great cradles of British rock music, the 2Is Coffee Bar and Liverpool's Cavern Club, sold nothing stronger than coffee, cola and orange juice, meaning teenagers had to enjoy themselves stone cold sober. If you wanted a 'drink' drink you got it in a pub, but you had to be eighteen to do that and even then only 'piss artists' got pissed, and 'piss artist' in those days was not a description to be proud of.

When (or why) it became de rigueur to get rat-arsed as a matter of policy I have not the slightest glimmer of an idea, but since the only people who benefit from it are the booze industry and the government, the conspiracy theorist in me suspects… well, some sort of conspiracy. The booze industry benefits from increased profits, the government benefits from increased tax revenue and a population that's pissed half the time and hence less likely to think about anything else, it's a win/win situation.

That's the reason there is so little jazz around now – jazz audiences don't drink enough. Put on a rock night, pop night, dance night, disco night, karaoke night, any kind of night and the punters will drink a lot, or more than that, because part of the reason for going to those nights is to get pissed. Jazz lovers, on the other hand, tend to go for the music, the bastards, and will often make a couple of drinks last all evening. So you do the maths and out goes the jazz which means the choice of music is based on how pissed the punters will get, and if that's not a fine way to choose music I don't know what isn't.

As for the drugs, well we need an intelligent discussion about those. Some are fine, I'm sure, some are fucking lethal, but like I say we need an intelligent discussion to sort that out and to have an intelligent discussion you need intelligent people. Now, where the hell are we going to find any of those?

The Great Will...

I was still seventeen when I got a call, out of the blue, from my cousin Ted who worked as a car park attendant in Soho. One of his regulars, Wee Willie Harris, had just got back from South America and needed a guitar player, Ted told me, and he had recommended me. I knew Willie was a star, and though I wasn't familiar with his work I'd read somewhere that John Lennon and Paul McCartney had queued up for his autograph at the Liverpool Empire, and if that wasn't recommendation enough I don't know what was. More to the point, Willie was *pro*. So, with some trepidation (I'd heard that Soho was full of weirdos and gangsters) I drove into town the next day to meet Willie and audition, trying to reassure myself on the way that all the talk of villains and hidden dangers was nonsense.

There was no reply when I rang the bell of Willie's flat above the 2Is Coffee Bar in Old Compton Street, and Ted said I should ring the bell underneath. This I did. The door was opened by a seven-foot-tall Bigfoot lookalike with a huge forehead, long matted hair and a voice that made the bloke who does the movie trailers sound like Joe Pasquale. I think my entire nervous system went into meltdown, but I must have said something cogent because it pointed to the Act One Scene One coffee bar over the road and it was there that I met Willie.

Call me naïve, but at that age I thought stars always looked like stars and at first I didn't notice him at all. In fact it was only when a little unshaven derelict in the corner said 'You

Ted's cousin are you?' that I realised it was him. I sat down, and without much preamble he began to ask me if I knew songs like 'Row, Row, Row', 'Get Out and Get Under' and 'Cry'. I had heard them all but I had never played any of them before, but this was where those years of ear training kicked in because, as long as it wasn't jazz, if I'd heard a song before I kinda knew the chord sequence instinctively.

So I responded in the affirmative, though I couldn't understand why he was asking. I knew Wee Willie Harris as a dyed-in-the-wool (and in the hair) rocker and rockers these weren't. Anyway he seemed satisfied, and pausing only while I retrieved my guitar and amp from the car he led me to a little basement club for my audition. Waiting there were Willie's manager Les Bristow, bassist Brian Gregg and drummer Tony Crombie. Hmmmm…

I say 'hmmmm…' because, though I didn't fully appreciate it at the time, I was in exalted company. Willie had, of course, been a name for years and star of TV's 'Six Five Special'. Famous for his shocking pink hair (gone by then - the pink, not the hair) he'd topped the bill with Cliff, toured with Buddy Holly and been mates with Gene Vincent (they once went to the ballet together, he told me, how rock 'n' roll is that?) Bassist Gregg had been with Johnny Kidd and the Pirates, played on 'Shakin' All Over' with them and on 'Telstar' with the Tornados. And Crombie was one of England's top jazz drummers and founder of one of Britain's first rock 'n roll bands The Rockets. And then there was me, eighteen months out of school, green as grass, twice as shaky and far from sure what I was getting myself into.

So, the audition began, turned into a rehearsal, and before I knew it I had agreed to meet them all next morning to begin a four-week stint on the road. Which presented me with a problem because the VIPs had gigs lined up too, and I have always prided myself on my sense of loyalty. Still, the word 'pro' was too seductive to resist and after the gig I told them. It's the only time I've ever let anyone down that way and it was horrible.

The next morning, still far from certain what I was getting into, I got into a minibus and we set off for Manchester. It occurred to me that despite doing five years of geography at school I had no idea where Manchester was. Or Leeds. Or Bristol or anywhere else in Britain. What the fuck were they teaching us and why? Surely you'd start from where you were and work outwards wouldn't you? No, apparently you wouldn't.

Any road up, all the way to Manchester Willie talked to me. Not to explain or clarify the act – I'd learned that the previous day. (You know it amazes me now that I learned an hour-and-a-quarter act from scratch in one afternoon; I don't know a seventeen-year-old now who could learn it in a month, but they don't learn the same way we did. Progress, eh?) No, Willie spent the time telling me about people in different parts of the country and illustrating with Scouse, Geordie, Scottish and various other accents, all of which were Greek to me. He acted no more like a star than he had the day before, and between that and the odd assortment of material I'd learned I was having serious second thoughts.

He did, however, explain one thing that I remember, and remember verbatim – his philosophy on women. It ran thus 'I find out if it fucks, and if it don't, bollocks to it'. I'm not sure which of Shakespeare's sonnets he got it from, but it was of no use to me anyway for reasons previously delineated. Still, good of him to share, I thought.

We were to do the act I'd learned three times that night in three different venues – the Levenshulme and Devonshire sporting clubs and the Cabaret Club in Manchester. The Lev was a vast barn of a place and packed with people. I set up my gear and stood waiting on stage, still wondering what the hell I was doing there, then someone announced 'Ladies and gentlemen, Wee Willie Harris' and to my shock and amazement a star burst out onto the stage and proceeded to tear the audience apart. It was mesmerising. He was fantastic, this little bloke, attacking every bit of his act with a gusto and charisma I didn't know existed, and that voice – gobsmacking. Within seconds all my doubts had been dispelled and he left that audience screaming for more. I couldn't believe it.

Thus I learned my first professional lesson – stars only have to dress and act like stars when they're 'on'. When they're off they can just be themselves. In fact real stars are like that instinctively, I've found. Only the tossers dress and act like stars all the time, which is how you can tell they're tossers. You can't tell truly great performers until they start to perform. Before and afterwards they're just people.

Willie had a strange relationship with his manager, Les Bristow, because although it was Will who sold the act on stage it was Les who designed it using a mental 'graph' idea of his own. He tried to describe it to me once – it was all a matter of highs and lows, placing the right songs in the right places. I was only able to grasp the bare bones of it but I got the message that if anything was out of place the whole thing would collapse. Clever stuff.

He also told me 'Other managers will tell you not to try to upstage the star but just stand at the back and play, but I tell you to try and nick the show off Willie every night because if he sees you doing that it will make him work harder', a ploy which I suspect would have got right up some performers noses, but Les knew Willie and Les was right. His best piece of advice, though, was probably 'everyone in England is an expert in two businesses - their own and ours', a sagacious piece of sarcasm I've never found cause to argue with.

Willie worked full weeks rather than one-nighters, though we did do a ten-day run of them once for an agent named Roy Tempest, who lent us one of his minibuses for the purpose. It had his name right along both sides and it was good of him to take the blame, frankly, as it was the sort of thing you'd lend someone if you *wanted* them to get arrested.

It had no tax disc, this thing, no number plates (front or rear), no tread on any of the tyres and every time you filled up with petrol you had to fill up with oil too. It wouldn't go up gradients on the motorway in anything higher than second gear, and the only way to get it up hill was for everyone but the driver to get out and walk. These days you'd get about fifteen years for driving a van like that, and I'm not sure it wasn't largely responsible for global warming.

I can't remember all the acts we worked with during those ten days, but I do remember that one of the gigs was at the Goldhawk Social Club in Shepherd's Bush because our support act that night was The Who. I kid you not. They hadn't made it at the time, obviously, but they were fantastic and we watched their entire set. The audience, however, ignored them and ran to the front when we came on because we were top of the bill. Every support band on earth knows exactly what I'm talking about.

I didn't understand it at the time, but I've since realised that most English people are incapable of judging music and have to be told what they should or shouldn't like before committing themselves. That night we were the stars so they ignored The Who. Six months later The Who had had a hit record, which meant we would have been supporting them and it would have been the other way round.

We talked to the chaps after the gig, and they told us they were so sick of being ignored they were going to buy some outlandish clothes, play as loudly as possible and smash up the gear at the end of a gig just to get some notice taken of them. It worked, but I think Townsend's songs and the band's recordings had something to do with it. I mean, 'My Generation'? Come on, what a track. And 'Won't Get Fooled Again'? Own up.

As I was saying, we normally worked full weeks with Willie and usually two shows a night, one at a social club and another later at a night club. The night clubs were often pretty swish, the social clubs neither one nor the other, but most of them were huge and they were packed every night of the week from 7 to 11pm with enthusiastic punters, most of whom, judging by the car parks, arrived in pretty new cars.

They made a fortune, some of these clubs, and being non-profit-making they could plough this back in booking the biggest acts of the day like Shirley Bassey and Tony Bennett. One of them actually made so much money in one year they had to give £100,000 back to the punters as a dividend. Now, I've heard politicians recently say that we all have much more 'disposable income' now than we had in the 1960s, but if you take a look at the equivalent clubs today you'll be forced to wonder what we're disposing of it on instead. Wasting it on bills and mortgages probably.

Playing such a wide variety of material was preparing me for future endeavours, and it wasn't just songs – Willie did impressions, too, each of which needed an appropriate snippet of music, and we did a band feature in the middle of the show too. Being a trio, I had to make the guitar fill in for the missing horns, piano or strings on the originals, which gave me great training in texturing, and doing a 'dead segue' act (no stopping) taught me to play under extremely adverse conditions. I've played the whole act with a top string missing, which meant having to re-think every chord and phrase on the spot; I've played the entire act with a hole in the end of my left-hand index finger, the result of a slip during a rushed pre-gig repair job; and, for one memorable week, I went on stage with eight blood-soaked stitches in the top of my shaven head, the result of trying to jump into the side door of a Ford Transit and missing. If only I'd had a Rubette hat…

I learned something else too - rhyming slang don't travel. I'd grown up with it and assumed it was a nationwide sport, but it turned out Northerners didn't speak it at all. So what, you may say? Well, it meant that we could talk about people in front of them and as long as we kept a straight face we could have been speaking Aramaic. Thus you could stand next to a well-endowed young lady and declare 'pipe the thruppenies on this Richard' without getting thumped by anyone. OK, not an earth-shattering accomplishment, but handy. And, to top it off, playing with Crombie taught me about swing because God, could he swing!

I was at his house one day when the phone rang; Crombie answered it, came back and asked how I'd fancy playing 'live' on Radio Caroline with American jazz organist Jimmy Smith. Now Radio Caroline was, I believe, the first pirate radio ship in Britain, and pirate radio transformed broadcasting. For the first time we had 24-hour pop music, and not just the singles the record companies wanted to plug but B-sides and album tracks too, in fact whatever the DJ fancied playing he played.

More than that, though, because if the DJ didn't like the track he'd just played he would say so. I mean, honestly, real opinions. It don't seem feasible now when everything is 'brilliant and amazing' however crap it is, but pirate DJs really did call a spade a spade. It's left me with a real problem, to be honest, because I always want to point out to DJs today that a third-rate record by four blokes from Accrington or some bird from Stoke is not 'amazing' in any dictionary definition of the word, nor (probably) 'brilliant'. The universe is 'amazing', Jimi Hendrix was 'amazing'. The only 'amazing' thing about most pop records is that they get played on the radio at all, and that ain't 'brilliant' in anyone's book.

Anyway the idea of seeing Radio Caroline in the flesh was a real thrill, and as for Jimmy Smith, well he was *the* jazz organist in the world at that time so 'yes' was the answer, and I tell you I'd never felt anything swing like that. I was out of my depth with him and Crombie obviously, but it was a terrific experience and the only time anyone played 'live' on a pirate ship apart from Blackbeard's concertina player.

I loved Tony Crombie, as a bloke and a musician, but I have one enormous bone to pick with him and it wasn't even really his fault. I was practising one day in the digs when Crombie stuck his head round the door and asked what I was doing. 'Practising' I said. He scowled. 'You've already got as much technique as you're ever going to need' he said, 'get your head into some harmony' and with that he walked away. Now to me, in them days, 'harmony' meant two or more people singing together in... well, in harmony, so I had no idea what he was talking about and Crombie, the bastard, didn't tell me.

What he meant by 'harmony', I discovered much, much later, was chord makeup and chord sequences, and I now know he was absolutely right – we all have as much technique as we're ever going to have by the time we reach our late teens or early twenties, any progress we make after that depends on our understanding of harmony. If we learn that we can go on improving for several thousand years, if we don't we stay about the same for twenty-odd years and then get worse. Believe me, I've seen it happen.

My 'bone' with Crombie is that if he'd told me what he meant at the time I'd have been a much better player much sooner and saved myself a lot of disappointment and frustration on the way. Of course he obviously didn't know I didn't know what he meant, if you know what I mean, so the problem was mine, not his, but since I found out what he meant I've tried to share the observation with everybody else *and* tell them what it means too. And d'you know what? Most of them don't know what I mean, know what I mean? Still, it keeps me off the streets, eh.

One of the things about working full weeks in strange towns (and some English towns were very strange) was the opportunity – nay, the necessity – to find something to do during the day, but that was easier then than it is now because every town in those days was different. The layout was different, the shops were different and there were a lot of eccentric little stores to find eccentric little bits and pieces in. This was pre The Antiques Roadshow, too, which meant most towns had lots of little junk shops full of antiques. We don't have them any more – what we have now are 'antique' shops full of junk and it's not the same.

In an effort to kill time Willie and I became regular moviegoers too. Most big towns boasted two or three cinemas back then, and as it was the heyday of Hammer Films, which both of us liked, we took in a lot of them. And many of them – 'The Pit and The Pendulum', 'The Fall of the House of Usher', 'The Masque of the Red Death', 'The Raven' - bore the legend 'based on a story by Edgar Allen Poe'. So when I came across a copy of 'Tales, Poems and Essays' I bought it.

Now, I have to say that Poe is not the ideal reading material for a depressive, obsessed as he was with blood, torture, cruelty, insanity and premature burial. It's a bit like using 'Airport' as an in-flight movie. But… Poe got me reading, something I'd only done before with musical biogs and histories, and once I'd started with him I naturally found people like Nathaniel Hawthorn, Algernon Blackwood, Ray Bradbury and, better still, Arthur Conan Doyle, because that meant Sherlock Holmes and he meant deductive reasoning.

I loved the Holmes stories, like ya do, but it was the concept of deductive reasoning that changed my life – the notion that once you've eliminated the impossible whatever's left, however improbable, must be the truth. I've applied it myself ever since, to a thousand different little problemettes, and it's been a Godsend. (I found out much later that Taoism expounds the similar 'observe, deduce, apply' principle, and that works too). Neither is 'scientific' in the usual sense of the word, but used conscientiously they answer many of the questions science can't. Professor Dawkins.

Being with Willie I became a well-travelled gentleman too. We worked pretty well all over England and Wales, we toured Germany and France and, courtesy of Combined Services Entertainments, half way around the world. We did shows on snow-covered mountains, in Middle Eastern deserts and in the jungles of Borneo, and when Crombie left the band I took over as leader. It was graft, but I was learning and I was *pro*. Very pro.

I have three particular reasons for remembering the first time I went abroad with Willie. The first was a sign on the autobahn in Germany for a place called Ausfahrt, or should I say a series of signs as there seemed to be one at every turn-off. This suggested that Ausfahrt was a huge town and I couldn't believe I'd never heard of it. Ausfahrt, in case you're wondering, means 'way out'. The second was an autobahn service station. We'd stopped in plenty of motorway services in England and they were all terrible. They looked awful, you went in feeling hungry, came out feeling nauseous, and the service was begrudging at best. The German one was welcoming, comfortable and smart, and the food was great. So this is Europe, I thought, we could learn a thing or two from this. I'm still waiting.

The third reason was far more significant, because like most first-time-abroad Brits I carried a kind of 'two world wars' mentality around with me. It wasn't seriously xenophobic or nationalistic, just… well, just what we did (and probably still do), basically tongue-in-cheek but still thick. Any bahn up, we got talking to a German bloke one night in a bar in Frankfurt and he started recounting his experiences in North Africa during the war. He was in tanks, his best mate was in the tank next door and when it was hit by a shell he heard his mate screaming as he burned to death. And I thought 'we did that'. It was a thought that had never really occurred to me before and it changed my mind about everything.

For reasons I cannot now remember, Willie and the band once travelled to Europe by train. This reminds me of two things – the journey home, which was assuredly the worst journey I ever experienced and more fraught with incidents than a decent film, and the bloke who did the passenger announcements at Paddington Station. I never met him, but his announcements made me laugh so much he became something of a hero.

How? I hear you ask. Well, whether it was company policy or his way of taking the piss I've no idea, but every word of his announcements was crystal clear except the destinations, which were completely indecipherable. I could demonstrate this much better verbally than in writing, but as you're not here and I'm not… well, you know. So I'll do the best I can. Imagine you are waiting at Paddington station, there's a click and you hear '**THE TRAIN NOW STANDING AT PLATFORM FOUR WILL CALL AT** *FLOXSHE, GLOOMLUL, BROMOONSAL, CASHRELMUM, FLOMBUNT* **AND ALL STATIONS TO** *SHKERBZ'*. And he did the same thing every time. Brilliant.

What? Oh the return trip…well, OK but I'll have to keep it brief or I'll need another book. We were in Frankfurt at the end of a tour, with one last gig to do before we caught the 8am train home from Frankfurt station. Unfortunately, the gig was in Nuremberg (I don't know how far that is exactly but it's a fucking long way) so we had no choice but to do the gig and come straight back again. This we did, arriving back at Frankfurt station with about five minutes to spare.

Les (who had already flown home, the bastard) had told us not to register the equipment on the train, as that way we could take it on as hand luggage and keep an eye on it. So we loaded it all on a trolley and took it to a guard's van, where the guard asked to see our registration papers. Willie told him we didn't have any and the guard said the gear couldn't go on the train without them. Willie started to argue with him, telling him we didn't register the gear when we brought it from England, but the guard would have none of it. Then Willie spotted another guard's van right at the other end of the train. 'Bring it up here' he said, and we dutifully dragged the trolley after him.

But that guard wouldn't let it on either. Willie started arguing again, we started laughing, and the more annoyed he became the more hysterical we got. Hysteria often broke out amongst us if things went wrong when we were particularly knackered, so we used to call them the 'hysterical miseries', shortened for tax purposes to the 'HMs'.

After five minutes of this Willie barked 'bring it down here' and once more we dragged the trolley the full length of the train, but the first guard still wouldn't let it on and Willie was now losing what was left of his rag. 'Don't fuck me about' he was yelling, 'I've got a fucking gig in Birmingham tomorrow' by which time we were rolling about helpless on the floor. We had now held the train up for about ten minutes and eventually Willie was forced to part with some folding to register the gear and get it on board.

We followed it onto the train, only to find that it was so packed with passengers there was not a seat left vacant, which meant we were faced with standing all the way to Ostend. I don't know how far that is, but it's a fucking long way. I asked Willie if he was sure the gear was going to be OK and he told me he had asked someone and been told it would be fine. I asked him who he'd asked and he pointed to a restaurant steward. I was far from reassured.

With no seats available we took it in turns to sit on our drummer Jeff Lawrence's record player in the aisle by the door, but I was so tired I eventually tried to get some sleep by hooking my arms through some brass rails and hanging there like a fucking bat.

Eventually the train stopped at Aachen (on the German-Belgian border, I think) and was about to set off again when our bassist, Roger Sutton, spotted all our precious gear outside on the platform. Panic, Mr Mainwaring. Willie, it seems, had only registered it that far, so we delayed the train again while more loot changed hands and our gear was brought back aboard. With all the delays we got to Ostend with only minutes to spare to catch the ferry, which meant we had to run for it carrying all our gear by hand. I don't know how far we had to run exactly, but it was a fucking long way.

Ostend was packed with passengers, but Willie and I finally managed to find the ferry. Unfortunately we'd lost Roger and Jeff in the process, so we told the purser he'll have to wait as we had their tickets and shot off to find them. While we were looking for them they found the ferry, but couldn't get on it as we had the tickets. So they went looking for us. You still with me?

Eventually we all got to the boat, which left fifteen minutes late because of us. The train journey from Dover to London seemed to take an eternity, and by the time we arrived we only had two or three hours to spare before Les was due to pick us up to take us to Birmingham. This meant there was no time to go home, so we hung around, knackered, until Les arrived. Off we went to Birmingham, where we checked into the digs, grabbed a bite to eat, set up the gear at the club and suddenly we were back on stage again having not slept, to all intents and purposes, for three days. All we wanted to do was get the gig over with and get our heads down.

We managed fine for a while, then a drunk started shouting. Nothing coherent, you understand, just a sort of 'woehgadbbushooo' every couple of minutes. Willie, trooper that he was, tried to ignore it and managed until he was half-way through his Jimmy Saville impression, at which point he cracked. 'Why don't you fuck off'! he shouted at the drunk, ironically still in his Jimmy Saville voice, and the whole place fell silent. Well, this was the '60s and you didn't tell someone to 'fuck off' from the stage in those days.

The management immediately sprang into action and ejected the drunk, but Willie was mortified. He'd never sworn on stage before, and proceeded to go into a full and heartfelt apology to the rest of the audience while we, so exhausted by then that we had a terminal case of the HMs, almost died laughing that silent laugh you have to adopt in the face of such situations, all tight lips, weak knees and bloodshot, tear-stained faces. I think it sapped the final dregs of energy we had, but it put the final full-stop to the worst journey I think any of us had ever had. I just wish you could have been there. You could have carried some of my stuff.

It was on one of Willie's CSE tours that I got paralytic for the first and only time in my life. We'd played the last of a run of gigs in Cyprus and we had a little party to say 'thanks' to the RAF blokes who had helped us hump the gear in and out. As usual I was down in the dumps and tried to alleviate it by drinking whisky sours, but the whisky ran out before the dumps did and I went on to brandy instead. The next thing I knew I was being carried into the lift. I remember falling between the two beds in our room, and the next moment I was taking a leak in the toilet and wondering why they had put a light fitting on the wall in front of me. It took me a while to realise I was lying on the floor and the next thing I knew it was morning. We had to take a flight to North Africa that morning, and though I had no headache my stomach was in turmoil the whole way and I vowed to myself there and then 'never again'. I know everybody says it but I meant it and I've never done it since.

I did get sick again, though, during a tour of the Middle East, and I do mean sick – the full Montzuma's revenge including frequent trips to the kahzi with a shocking case of the runs. Again we had a flight the next day, and when we reached our destination I went straight to the MO. He gave me two tablets and a little glass of medicine and told me to take it all and lie down. This I did. Five minutes later I was in the khazi again and I threw up what felt like the entire contents of my stomach, liver, spleen, chest and both elbows. Knackered, I lay down again and five minutes later I was completely cured. I couldn't believe it. I'd been to doctors in England with stomach problems and they'd fixed them eventually but this was like a miracle. I guess in the forces they take the 'kill or cure' approach but I couldn't have been more grateful to that MO.

It was on another one of these tours that we found ourselves in Aden, a place plagued with sporadic terrorist activity, much of which centred on the main road that ran parallel with the docks and which the British forces were there to patrol. The forces were a pleasant lot (to us, anyway) and one afternoon Willie and I were invited by one of the officer's wives to tea at their home. She would pick us up from our hotel, she said, and bring us back afterwards, so Willie and I got ourselves dressed up as best we could and waited for her to arrive. I had recently acquired a tasty white jacket decorated with red and blue stripes, so I put that on. Any road, she duly arrived in a two-seater sports car. No problem,

I said, it was a nice sunny day, I would perch up on the back. It was only when we turned onto the main dock road that I realised I was perched up on the back of a sports car travelling along the most dangerous road in town in broad daylight in a red, white and blue jacket like a target in a bloody funfair. The journey probably only took ten minutes but I swear I was ten years older when we got to the other end.

When I mentioned this to the officer he waved my worries aside with a flourish. 'Don't worry about that' he said, 'these people are hopeless. They kill themselves more often than they damage us' and he told me of a local man who had been forced by terrorists to drive a car full of primed explosives and park it outside a large hotel. 'This man couldn't find anywhere to park' he said, 'so he drove round and round looking for a space until the car exploded with him in it. Hopeless'! I could see his point, but it didn't make the journey back any more relaxing.

Much more relaxing was a month I spent with Willie in Berlin, partly because it was a full month in the same town and partly because it was a month in the same club, the New Eden Saloon, which meant no humping gear every night, danke very schöen. And we only had to play one spot a night, which meant we were effectively working for just 90 minutes a day. This being the 60s, the same couldn't be said for other British bands, most of whom were, at the time, doing something like eight *hours* a night at other German clubs. Cheers, Will.

Berlin (or 'West Berlin' as it was called then) was a strikingly beautiful, upbeat place, full of colour and boogying like everywhere else in western Europe in the mid 60s. The Beatles were even more in evidence there than they were in England, and I bought a German-label copy of 'Rubber Soul' from a record shop on the Kurfürstendamn. Bizarrely, though, many of the walls in the town were still pock-marked with bullet holes, presumably ours, and of course there was *the* Wall. We went to look at it, naturally, and in a fit of uncharacteristic courage I agreed to go with the others through Checkpoint Charlie into the Eastern sector.

It was an eye-opener. Where West Berlin sparkled with every colour in the rainbow, East Berlin was uniformly grey. The streets were grey, the buildings were grey, the cars were grey, the people were grey, everything was grey except the tea, but they made up for that by making it lukewarm. I'm not particularly anti-communist, but if East Berlin was anything to go by I'd avoid it if I were you. I was working for the Burnley Express when the wall came down, and I couldn't have been more delighted. Mind you, everyone was delighted by that so I don't know why I said it.

This will sound rather petty after all that, but I saw the most amazing car I'd ever seen when I was in Berlin, parked right outside the New Eden Saloon. It was a deep cherry red colour with gorgeous ivory white upholstery and fascia and it was at least twenty feet long. Despite this, it was a two-seater, the rest of the length taken up by an enormous bonnet and boot. (Sorry, it was an American car, 'hood' and 'trunk', my apologies for being so parochial). Any road up, while I was watching (and wondering why anyone would need a ten-foot trunk) a bloke exited the club, got in the car and pressed a button, at which point the trunk swung open and a hard top emerged, lowered itself onto the centre compartment and the bloke started the engine and sped off. I wanted one. Still do.

If you were looking for somewhere as unlike West Berlin as possible you needed to look no further than Borneo. (Actually you couldn't look much further – it's a long way away). We were there courtesy of the RAF, some of whom were ensconced in fairly comfortable quarters near towns but some of whom were barely ensconced in anything but. You had to be there to believe it, but we were.

We played a couple of these places, each of which consisted of nothing more than a deforested hill in the middle of impenetrable jungle, with wooden stakes and barbed wire surrounding the base and sandbag-lined trenches at the top. They looked like sets for 'Camp on Blood Island'. These trenches the RAF chaps were obliged to call home for up to three months at a stretch, and the officers' mess was five sheets of corrugated iron with a door cut in one side. Such opulence! We were flown into these delightful bijou resorts in Belvedere helicopters, double-rotor noise makers the RAF chaps loved to tell us were nicknamed 'widow-makers', which didn't bother me too much as I wasn't married at the time.

We did the shows on makeshift platforms, and I have to say the reception we got was fantastic. Well it would be, wouldn't it? We were told that the jungle (and there was hundreds of square miles of it in every direction) was more or less impenetrable - 'like a mattress' they said – and that, as an exercise in jungle survival, a small group of RAF chaps had been sent out into it to find their way back to town. They disappeared for months, presumed lost, and when they finally did emerge they were like wild men and had to be sent home for a long course of psychiatric treatment. So if you ever find yourself in Borneo, don't go down to the woods – you're sure of a big surprise.

Of course not all Borneo was quite so inhospitable. On a rare day off, a couple of RAF chaps loaded up a boat with Coca Cola and orange juice and took us up the river to see one of the local villages, which consisted of little wooden houses built on stilts out into the water. We stopped at one of these and met the village chief, who happily accepted our meagre refreshments and, in return, sent his kids scurrying like lizards up the trees to cut us down some coconuts. He then showed us round his house and introduced us to his three wives, his first (who had been promoted to housework duties) his second (who took care of the children) and his latest, who took care of his carnal requirements. It wasn't an arrangement that would have delighted Germaine Greer, but it suited him (and apparently his wives, who got on with each other well) and he couldn't have been more charming.

You know, the mystery of how people lead such different lives to our own never fails to amaze me. And here's a case in point. We were touring North Africa, and in flying over the desert we spotted the occasional tent, all on its own in the middle of nowhere. So later, when some RAF blokes asked if we'd like to see one of them close up we said 'yes, we'd like to see one of them close up'. We all got in a Land Rover and drove, quite fast and for quite a long time, until one of these isolated tents hove into view.

It was a big 'un, right enough – a large detached property in a few million acres, with delightful views of a few more million acres and within easy reach of... well, that's the point. It didn't appear to be within any sort of reach of anything apart from sand and rocks. No Asda, no shops and, as far as I could see, no water, yet there was a full family happily living in and around it, and I mean happily, in that they were wreathed in the kind of smiles I've never seen in Asda.

They had a couple of goats, quite a lot of cooking pots and a great deal of soft furnishings, but apart from that, very little. No telly, no radio, no phone, no car, no camel that I could see, yet there they were looking happy and healthy. *HOW*? I couldn't ask because I didn't speak the language, and frankly it would have sounded patronising if I could. I could have done some research afterwards but I didn't. In a way I didn't want to know.

To me, the point was that they managed to live, and apparently live well, in conditions we would regard as completely untenable, which made the things we think are indispensable look very suspect. In the same way as we once lived well without Tesco and broadband, they managed without shops and water and I respected them enormously for it. Needless to say they managed without mortgages and electric bills too, and I envied them that. They were free agents as far as I could see, and how fab is that?

But I have to say, the most spectacular place I ever went with Willie was Masirah, a small island off the Persian Gulf which consisted of nothing but an RAF base and a local village. Again we did the show on a makeshift stage, and as we had a day to kill two RAF chaps asked if we would like to go fishing. Now I don't care for fishing, but as the alternative was four or five hours of fuck all I went along for the ride. Good move.

We set off in an RAF flat-bed truck, called in at the village to pick up the local fishing expert, then made our way to the beach. Now, you've seen beaches, right? You may even have seen beaches abroad. But you ain't seen nothing like this one. If ever there was a place that looked exactly like God made it, this was it. Acres of white, silver sand, hermit crabs running around free, and huge (I mean *huge*) upturned turtle shells, all empty as their contents had long since been devoured by something or other. Overhead the sky was an unbroken blue, birds wheeled in their hundreds and the sea was sparkling blue and clear as glass.

Of course it was like this because the only things on Masirah were the RAF base and the village. No hotels, no cafes or bars, no resorts. It would have been a millionaires' paradise, but they weren't allowed, and as you looked at it all you knew that one hotel, one bar, one café and the place would be fucked. You know that Eagles track 'The Last Resort', where he sings 'call some place paradise, kiss it goodbye'? Quite.

So what about the fishing, I hear you cry? Well, standing proud a few hundred yards off shore was a ship that had run aground on the coral some years before, and we were loaded onto a large inflatable landing craft and taken out to it, accompanied all the way by leaping, frolicking dolphins. The coral had ripped the bottom right out of the ship, so looking down into the hold was like looking into a natural aquarium, its clear water lit by a tropical sun. We saw shark, barracuda, stingrays and God knows what else.

We were then dispersed to various parts of the deck by the RAF blokes and given a length of line, a hook and some bait. 'Just drop it in the water and wait' they said. It wasn't a long wait – within minutes the water was thick with red sea bass, and we were pulling one out every couple of minutes. It was murder, I tell you, pure murder. After about half an hour we had a stack of fish at our feet, and the RAF guys started calling for us to take them to the poop deck at the stern of the ship.

This we did, and I swear I thought they were taking the piss when they took a rope with a butcher's hook tied to the end, skewered a complete 7lb bass and threw it over the side. They weren't joking. Ten minutes later we were looking at two enormous fish – as tall as me, I reckon – and to prove the point the RAF blokes put two beer cans end-to-end in the mouth of one of them. We were out about three hours all told, and got back to the RAF base with 350lb of fish.

Masirah, I believe, now has a full complement of hotels, bars and cafes, so I metaphorically kiss it goodbye. It's one of humanity's great ironies that when you find a place you wish everyone could see you know that if they did they'd wreck it.

James Bond was a recent phenomenon around that time, and it was at RAF El Adem (in Libya, I believe) that I first saw 'Goldfinger'. I mention it because it's intriguing how knowing a lot about something can spoil your enjoyment of a film. As a muso I'm often annoyed by actors pretending to play the piano or the cello without bothering to even try to attempt to make it look reasonably realistic. I mean, come on, chaps, you're being paid here. It *can* be done – look at Ralph Macchio in 'Crossroads' or Geoffrey Rush in 'Shine'. I'm furious, too, when biopics get things wrong, like showing Gary Busey playing a 1970s Fender in 'The Buddy Holly Story', I mean, this is basic stuff here, do some research, people.

So, there I am watching 'Goldfinger' and loving it, as is everyone else, until the final scene, where Goldfinger shoots the window out of the plane, it hurtles towards destruction and we cut to Bond and Pussy under a parachute on the beach, at which point the place erupted in cat-calls, jeering and general 'do me a favour' type piss-taking. Pilots, you see, all pilots who knew about such things. Note, if you will, that they didn't bat an eyelid over Oddjob's lethal bowler hat or Bond's under-wetsuit dinner jacket, presumably because they weren't tailors, milliners or divers, but a bit of OTT aeronauticals unleashed the dogs of derision. Like I say, we're all the same – just thank God we don't know more about more things or none of us would ever enjoy a movie again.

I learned a valuable lesson about timing when I was with Willie. Not *from* Willie exactly, but through him. It came about thus. Back in England, one of our best provincial mates was a comedian called Jerry Harris who was based at one of the major Manchester nightclubs. Jerry was both cockney and Jewish, which is the comic equivalent of having a master's degree and a doctorate, and whenever we were in town we'd call in on Jerry under the pretext of asking if he had any ideas for the act (we actually went for a fucking good laugh, which was guaranteed with him). So when Willie was offered a one-hour special by Granada TV he did the logical thing and suggested they get Jerry to compere it.

This they did, and on the day of filming Jerry came out, did his gags exactly as he'd always done and he wasn't funny. I was speechless. I thought perhaps it might be me so I paid more attention but nothing changed, then I noticed the cameras. Now I'd heard about timing and that the slightest thing could throw it off, and that was the only explanation I could come up with – the cameras were making him just nervous enough to throw off his timing and Bob wasn't his uncle any more, and we're talking *nanoseconds* here, not discernible by the eye or ear (or computer, I'm guessing) but enough to superglue the works. I've since come to realise that comic timing and musical phrasing are the same thing but I won't bore you with that now. I'll bore you with it later.

I learned another lesson with Willie one night, but this one I dismissed with contempt. It happened thus – Willie used to finish his act with the old Isley Brothers' steamer 'Shout', during which I usually played my arse off. On this particular night, though, I was feeling rather pissed off so instead of my usual noodlings I resorted to just hitting the strings of my guitar with my hand on the first beat of each bar and letting the chords ring. To my shock, I found people crowding around me afterwards telling me what a great player I was! Now there are plenty of guitar players who would have grabbed that lesson with both hands and made a career out of it, but I was so appalled by the public's ignorance I never did it again. Which proves two things – 1, the public do tend to be rather uninformed about the finer points of guitar playing; and 2, I was an idiot.

Some audiences, though, could be impossible to figure, and one of the most infamous amongst acts was the one that frequented the Southern Sporting Club in Manchester. I have to say that Willie always went down well there but it could be a graveyard for some, as the following tale will illustrate. There were two 'pretend American' acts around at the time, a country and western duo who wore cowboy outfits complete with stage Colt revolvers, and a bloke who dressed as a native American, feathered headdress and the lot, and did a knife-throwing/bow-and-arrow-shooting act. These two turns found themselves sharing the bill at the Southern one week, and having died the death for two or three nights came up with a scheme to 'wake the audience up'.

So the following night when the duo were in the middle of their act the Indian, as arranged, went to the back of the club and let loose an arrow which thudded into the backdrop behind them. They drew their Colts and started shooting and the Indian let rip back at them with a stage Winchester rifle.

This barrage went on until all three weapons were empty, and the consensus of opinion between the two acts afterwards was that none of the punters had even looked up from their beer. Now that's what you call 'a tough crowd'.

In our case, though, it had nothing on Thurnscoe. I'd been with Willie for a couple of years by the time we got to do a week at the Yorkshire town's brand new, purpose-built club, which boasted all mod cons including theatre flats, tabs and lights (none of which they knew how to use, by the way). We went on to a packed house on the Sunday night (as usual) and died, which was not usual at all. We came off, looked at each other, shook our heads and went back to the digs, confused but not downhearted. The following night we went on and died again.

I was sitting in the bar afterwards when the concert secretary, a big bloke called Ginger for obvious reasons, came over. 'All reet, lad'? he said. I confessed that I was not particularly all reet and explained why. Ginger got serious. 'Can you take some constructive criticism'? he said. I said it would be my pleasure, and he went on to explain that the audience did not understand Willie's act. They didn't understand his Johnny Ray impression, he said, or his Jimmy Saville (which God knows was obvious) and the old-time medley we did was 'old fashioned'. You may think that's the point of an old-time medley but the Thurnscoe crowd obviously didn't get the message.

Ginger went on to explain that instead of gradually building the act up to a climax we should come on full-tilt and gradually 'peter off' (his words, honest) and that we should turn down the amplifiers a bit. I naturally thanked him for his keen insights and went to tell Willie, who was a trifle nonplussed. It wasn't the first time Willie had been nonplussed, but this time I reckon he had good reason. 'So what do we do'? I said. 'Fuck it' said Willie, 'we'll just go on tomorrow, do an hour of rock 'n' roll and see what happens'.

So the next night we abandoned the act completely. Willie called 'Miss Ann, F' and we did that, then 'Long Tall Sally, G' and so on, and they loved it. So that's what we did for the rest of the week, but the mystery of why Thurnscoe, alone amongst clubs, could not understand Willie's act continued to puzzle and confuse us. Only on the Friday did someone point out that most people in Thurnscoe had never been as far as Doncaster, which was *eight miles* away. The problem had been one of parochialism, simple as. And yet every house in the town had a TV aerial.

Now TV is supposed to be the great eye-opener, the great educator and mind-broadener, but that experience taught me a lesson I've learned in other circumstances since, namely that – in the words of the great Sioux chief Sitting Bull – 'you are what's around you'. The stuff that emanates from a screen in the corner of the room comes a very poor second to that, and I suspect the same applies to computers. I mean, look how much more open-minded and intellectual we've all become since the internet. For more on this subject, read my new book 'Sarcasm for Beginners' available from all good recycling centres.

So, you may be asking, how was a fat kid with PTSD dealing with all this activity? Well, first I wasn't fat any more. Within four months of joining Willie I lost more than three stone. But I hadn't lost my sense of isolation. In the early days I was still noticeably depressive and when Willie stayed behind after the show gambling (he was an inveterate gambler then but quit completely later) and the others went to check out the talent I would go back alone to the hotel, quite often walking miles to get there.

I was once joined for part of the way on one of these midnight treks by a nice-looking woman who had been in the audience at the club. She was about forty, I reckoned, and we chatted amiably (don't ask me what about) until we reached her place, at which point she invited me in. In we went, but we hadn't got any further than the hall when her husband called to her from upstairs and she pushed me back out into the night and closed the door.

Now, call me Sir Thicko-Green or the Duke of Knobland if you will, but it was only then that it dawned on me that she might have had designs of an erotic persuasion on my person, designs only feasible in the event of her spouse being lost in the arms of Morpheus and curtailed, therefore, by his obvious consciousness. Yes, that's how fucked up I was. I didn't even know when I was being pulled. Of course in hindsight, if I had realised it and gone for it I might well have been beaten to a pulp by her husband, so ignorance might well have been bliss.

Speaking of which, I did finally achieve a romantic liaison, with one of the dancers on our first summer season, but as you might expect I was fucking hopeless. And you can take that remark whichever way you like. She was lovely and sweet too, but for all the use I was you might as well have asked me to pilot a space shuttle. I can believe my own ignorance because how could I be anything else but ignorant, but I can't believe that after all those years of celebate yearning I was totally unappreciative of what I had. Or, more accurately, what she had. The only concept I had of sex was fucking, and when she told me she was a virgin I refused to do that. The other means of sexual pleasuring I had no clue about so she got nothing out of it at all and I've felt guilty about it ever since. Mind you, she presumably knew nothing either or I would have thought she'd have put me straight.

Now if we'd both had access to on-line pornography... you see where I'm coming from here... if we'd had access to that kind of sexual information we'd both have been aware of all the possibilities and I might have made her very happy indeed. And there I rest my case.

Incidentally, Willie's co-star on that summer season (the Arcadia Theatre, Skegness for all you trivia fans) had been one of the biggest stars of variety in its heyday and was still performing like it at eighty – the magnificent Jimmy James. He worked little three-part patter sketches with two 'stooges' and we watched his act every night, twice a night, for about three months.

Some comedy is only funny once, maybe twice. After that you know what's coming. But Jimmy's material and performance were of another order altogether. It was funny, and continued to be funny like Mozart continues to be musical. In fact it was *so* funny that when his son, BBC producer James Casey, recreated one of his sketches on TV years later (the one about the man-eating lions in a cardboard box), I still laughed at it. And I'd seen it twice a night for three months. Now that's *funny*.

Poor old Jimmy collapsed during that season and never worked again (Norman Collier took over for the rest of the run) but I bet he's still getting laughs with that sketch in the vast eternal variety theatre in the sky. The sound you hear during thunder storms is God laughing at Jimmy James, and I bet they don't teach you that at Cambridge.

I bought my first car for that summer season. It was a Standard Vanguard and I think it cost me £60. It was black, with a great sloping back, a bench front seat, a three-speed column-change gearbox, a proper box-steel chassis and the horn was on a chrome ring inside the steering wheel, as on American cars of the day. In fact it looked a bit like the Buicks they used in the TV series 'Highway Patrol' and it weighed a ton. Actually more than a ton and a quarter, yet it had no power steering or power breaks, which meant it went like a rocket in a straight line but didn't like to go round corners or stop. Since both of these are kind of prerequisite in the average car journey you can imagine what fun I had driving it, but I loved it. In fact I'd love one now. Ideally with additional power steering and brakes.

I met a lot of great people during my time with Willie, most notably Lonnie Donegan. We actually stayed in the same hotel for a week in Roker, near Sunderland, and went to each other's shows, but I was too withdrawn to make as much of it as I'd have liked. I did ask him, though, to confirm or deny something I'd read in a Lon biography about Denny Wright. The book said that when Lonnie came back from promoting 'Rock Island Line' in America his new record label, Pye, wanted an album from him pronto. Lonnie replied that he had no band, but Pye told him to get one quick as the studio had already been booked.

So Lonnie called upon jazz mates Nick Nicholls (drums) and bassist Mickey Ashman, someone recommended a guitarist and on the appointed day three of them turned up at the studio ready to go. No guitarist, though. They waited for over an hour, but time was money in those days so when the studio manager said he knew a guitar player who might fit the bill they asked him to give the bloke a call.

Denny was in bed at the time and didn't have a guitar in the house, but he got up, put his clothes on over his pyjamas, borrowed a guitar from the nearest music shop, arrived at the studio and said 'what are you playing'? Lonnie told him, and Denny played the whole album by ear. And – and this is the point – played it brilliantly, so brilliantly that it was one of the biggest influences on my own playing back then.

Of course the story sounded too good to be true, a typical bit of music PR nonsense, but Lonnie confirmed it happened exactly as I'd read it. So when he and Denny Wright came to see our show and I got a compliment afterwards from Denny you can imagine how chuffed I felt.

I met Brian Gregg's old guvnor Johnny Kidd, too, when we gave him a lift back into London one night and he told us about his method of getting out of a management contract he'd been stuck in for years – 'I walked into his office, threw his typewriter through the window and told him he'd be next if my contract wasn't on the desk in five seconds'. It was.

Through Willie I also met Big Jim Sullivan, but not until 2002, which seems crazy considering how long we'd both been doing more or less the same thing. Jim was a member of the Krew Kats who backed Marty Wilde and also toured with Eddie Cochran, and we met when Willie was in Burnley in a show with Vince Eager – yes, the one the Vibratones had supported in Greenwich. The meeting was fairly brief and I only mention it to show Willie's amazing powers of diplomacy. We were in the Mechanics bar when Willie said 'you haven't met Jim, have you? Wait, I'll go and get him'. He came back five minutes later with Jim, who shook my hand and said 'Willie tells me you can blow me off the stage'. If you want to be embarrassed you can always rely on Will.

Oh, and I met John Lennon, backstage in Bradford during the Beatles' final tour. We were only playing the night club that week (no doubles) which meant we didn't start work till around 1am, so when we heard that the Beatles were coming to town Willie suggested we go and watch. There was a kind of unwritten law or 'professional courtesy' back then which allowed any pro in town into any place of entertainment in town, so we had no problem gaining entry to watch the Nashville Teens, Sounds Incorporated and Mary Wells rehearsing for the show before going backstage to say hello. If I sound cavalier about this you don't know me yet, 'cause I was as excited as a high court judge at a Cynthia Payne party.

There was still no sign of the Beatles, though, and when Willie said we should go back out front and find our seats I was more than a mite disappointed. We exited through the stage door, and as we stepped into the alley at the back a police van came flying in, the gates slammed shut behind it, and out of the van came the Beatles, running. It was like a scene from 'A Hard Day's Night'. To my amazement as they ran past us they all said 'hello Will' and the next thing I knew I was in a dressing room with my guvnor and John Lennon.

Willie introduced me and I shook his hand, but I couldn't say a word. I was in awe of Lennon and being in his presence did nothing to diminish that. He and Willie chatted like old mates for a while, then someone stuck his head round the door and said 'press conference in ten minutes, John'. John glowered. 'Tell 'em to fuck off' he said. We were stunned. Me and Will would have given our goolies for a press conference (well, one each) and we couldn't understand it. 'It's the same every day' said John, 'and they always ask the same questions, so now we always give them different answers'. I still didn't really understand it at the time, but I got a hint of what he meant when I was in the charts myself ten years later and there were times when I wanted to tell them to fuck off too.

We watched the Beatles perform that night, but 'watch' is the operative word because you couldn't hear anything over the screaming. I begged Willie to stop it but... As it turned out the bloke in front of us didn't even see anything as he had his face buried in his girlfriend's back while he held her up so she could scream at four other blokes. And they say men are selfish.

I not only played in every possible environment with Willie, we travelled in every kind of transport and worked on everything from makeshift stages to the Victoria Palace. If you wanted a fully-rounded education Harris University was the place to be, and to put the tin hat on it, Willie and I were the best of friends. We still are. In fact if it hadn't been for Shirle I'd probably never have left him.

I sometimes stayed with Will in his flat above the 2Is and the Soho I'd once been so scared of became like home. Texan wrestler Sky High Lee (the Bigfoot who'd opened the door for me, remember?) lived in the flat below with his 4ft 11" ex-stripper girlfriend and turned out to be a real sweetheart – never judge by appearances. We'd see the Rolling Stones in the Act One Scene One or Hank and Bruce browsing the music shops, and my proudest moment came when the barkers outside the strip clubs – 'twelve lovely girls, they're naked and they dance' – started ignoring me because I looked like a local.

Via Willie I learned that the 'night' people I'd been warned against talked more sense and understood life far better than the people I'd been told to listen to. This hit me most forcibly one night in a club in Newcastle when I'd only been with Willie for a few weeks. We had just finished the show and got changed, it was 3am, the punters had all gone, we got ourselves some drinks and sat down with the only people left in the place, i.e. the local underworld of villains and tarts.

I didn't join in the conversation – too shy – but I ear'oled it all and it was light years beyond the kind of stuff I'd heard at home or at school. Real, it was, and honest in a way only 'dishonest' people seem to be able to manage.

Discussing this with Willie and Les I was told that the West End had lost something valuable a few years earlier when a new law had taken the working girls off the streets. It was obviously designed to 'clean them up' (the streets, not the girls) but, according to the dynamic duo, had only succeeded in forcing the whole thing underground and giving much more power to the ponces and villains.

It had also had an adverse effect on the social atmosphere of the area, they said, as prior to that the local musicians and tarts would all wish each other 'good evening' and 'goodnight' by name as they passed each other, making for a very friendly environment. This would never have occurred to me if they hadn't said it, and I've been suspicious of 'clean-up' campaigns ever since. They might seem like a sound idea on paper (or in the paper) but then so did 'political correctness' and look at the mess *that's* left us in. (Anything that starts with the word 'political' has almost got to be a bad idea, hasn't it?)

Another thing which would never had occurred to me unless I'd experienced it myself is the loneliness of hotel rooms which, like any lesson worth learning, is only learnable by experience. It's no wonder so much extra-marital goes on 'on the road' because going back to an empty hotel room on your own night after night, week after week, really does become unbearable, to the point where you can't face opening the door. I know, it sounds like an excuse, but unless you've had to do it you'll never know, and here's a poignant case in point.

There was a comedian, I was told, who was married with kids and took it so seriously he didn't dream of cheating until one fateful night when the horror of another empty room led him to invite a young lady back with him. He only did it once, his wife found out and he lost the lot – wife, kids and house. I did it myself once, but I wasn't married at the time and yes, I was just as useless as the last time. Worse, in fact, as I don't think either of us came away satisfied.

Now, two things. One, however unbearable lonely hotel rooms were for me, I at least had the company of Willie & Co. the rest of the time – solo performers don't even have that. They spend all day, every day, on their own among strangers in strange towns, entertain them for an hour or so and then go back on their own to an empty room. In his book 'It's Not a Runner Bean' comedian Mark Steel reckons three or four days of it will start to send you loopy, and some people do it for years.

And two, not every wife reacts like that poor comedian's. There are some who know full well that their husbands are at it every night and simply don't care as long as he always comes back to them at the end. Such women are rare, I'm sure, but then life is always surprising.

Thinking back on it, the three or four years I spent with Willie were the most honest, truthful, enjoyable and informative years of my life. Of course being a kid, and a kid with PTSD, I didn't really appreciate it as much as I should have but there's no denying it now. While I couldn't do what he did, he showed me how it should be done and there's nothing unpleasant about going a storm every night, week after week either. Willie was one of the only people I've ever come across who could make the band he was working with play twice as well as it did without him. Like all the best lessons I've no idea how he did this, but however good the band was to start with he did it every time.

I only recorded with Willie three times but on two of those there were some interesting people on hand. For the first, on a track called 'Big Bad Wolf' (which I don't think was ever released back into the wild) we were joined in the studio by Tony Sheridan, the man who gave the Beatles their first recording sessions in Germany. And for the second, a track called 'Someone's in the Kitchen With Dinah', the backing singers were Madeleine Bell and Dusty Springfield. Honest guv. I can't remember why they did it but there's certainly no mistaking Dusty's voice. Fab, eh?

Bizarrely, Willie never had a hit record, even in his hey-day, which is why he's so seldom mentioned now. He just never had the right people around to advise him. Whenever I mention Cliff to him he says 'lucky boy' which, compared to Willie, Cliff was. He had Norrie Paramor as producer, his first guitarist (Ian Samwell) wrote his first big hit (Move It!) which was the first song he'd ever written, and after that he had Hank and Bruce. I'd call that lucky. I only ever had three great 'bosses' in my life and Willie was one of them. We actually called him 'the great Will', hence the title of this chapter.

I met Shirle, who it turned out hailed from Burnley, when she supported Willie at a club in Cardiff. All the acts shared the same farmhouse for the week and we used to give her a lift to the club and back every night so I got to know her pretty well, but I reckon we were both smitten on day one. It's day 16,800 now and we're still together so I think it will last.

Of course having met Shirle I started visiting Burnley socially, usually travelling up from London by coach whenever we had a week off. I did once get a lift up from Willie in his Triumph Spitfire after playing a week in Wales, but that turned out to be a big mistake because I had the keys of the band Volvo in my pocket and Volvos, apparently, are notoriously difficult to get into and start with no keys. The AA managed it eventually, I was told later in a series of threatening and disgruntled voices, after which no one spoke to me at all for three days.

Meeting Shirle's mum and dad I fell pretty much in love with them too. Ern was a typical bloke, insofar as it was work, tea on the table, down to the club, back (pissed) for a cup of tea and then bed, but underneath was a real warmth and affection and a pretty keen mind. He had actually taken part in the D-Day landings; he didn't talk about it much, but what he did say told me it had left a lasting impression on him, which is hardly surprising. I reckon it would have put me in Broadmoor.

Lil, on the other hand, was an angel pure and simple. I have only known one other person so dedicated to looking after everyone but herself (my aunt Vera) and even in her later years, when she was plagued with the illness that killed her, I never heard her complain. The one thing I'm certain of is that no one will ever be able to say that about me. Naturally having met Shirle I didn't fancy being on the road and away from her for weeks on end, and that's when I called it quits with Willie. I think he managed without me.

I really can't let this section end without mentioning Willie's fishing. It's a subject that merits a book on its own, frankly, but I'll confine myself to one story that kind of sums up all the rest. We were on Gan Island in the Maldives, which in those days was occupied only by the locals and the RAF. Willie had gone fishing earlier that morning and when he came back he had half a dozen good sized fishes tied to his rod. When we asked them where he'd got them from he told us he'd caught them, but we didn't believe that for a second because Willie couldn't catch fish. If he'd told us he'd flown to the moon on gossamer wings we'd have believed him sooner because Willie couldn't catch fish. His manager, Les, told us that when Willie went fishing in Deal in Kent he would buy some fish on the way back, but there was no fishmonger's on Gan Island and Willie continued to insist he'd caught them. It was a case worthy of Sherlock Holmes, but he was fictional too.

We came back to England and were still pondering the mysterious Maldive affair when Willie announced that he'd got his film back from the developers (he was an avid 8mm home movie maker) and suggested we rent a projector and watch them in the digs. This we did, and after numerous shots of camels and aeroplanes up came the footage from Gan Island – sun, sea, sandy beaches, fruit bats, and fish flying out of the water onto the dock as the RAF blasted the harbour. And you know, Willie still insisted he caught those fish. And technically he probably did. On the way down.

NB: Remember Masirah? 350lbs of fish with just lines and bait? Willie had a rod, weights, sinks, floats, a peg to hold the rod to the rail, a bell to let him know when he had a bite, all the gear, in other words, and where we were just dropping our lines, Willie was casting. It was pointed out to him that a: we were already half a mile off shore and b: he was casting *over* the fish crowding round the ship, but this deterred him not a whit. Between us we caught 350lbs of fish, Willie caught one, about three inches long. And he still insisted he was the only one doing it right.

One quick story before I move on. I was at home one day when the phone rang. I answered it (call me old fashioned) and it was Jeff Lawrence, Willie's drummer at the time. We chatted for a while, then he asked me what my mum was doing and I told him she was cooking the dinner. 'Tell her I can smell the steak' he said, so I called to my mum and told her Jeff said he could smell the steak. 'I'm not cooking steak' said my mum, 'it must be the chops he can smell'. Mums, eh?

Back in London, unemployed, I accepted an offer to put a house trio into the Cromwellian Club in Kensington, and that's when I realised how much things had changed while I'd been Willie-ing. People kept asking me why I didn't play like Eric Clapton, a fucking stupid question seeing as I wasn't Eric Clapton, and one that merited one of only two answers. Why should I? And/or why doesn't Eric Clapton play like me?

I didn't really know who Eric Clapton was, truth be told; all that John Mayall thing had happened while I was out of town with Willie, and we hardly saw any TV because we were working every night. So I was still listening to the Beatles, the Stones and the Who, and when I did listen to the 'hip' stuff of the day – blues and soul – I found it relatively uninspiring. This wasn't helped by being surrounded by idiots saying 'you gotta play the blues, man' when what they meant was 'you gotta have long hair, a Les Paul and a Marshall stack. Man'.

Let me make two observations here: 1, I am a natural-born trend-resister. Tell me what I 'should' be doing and I'll instinctively rebel against it and look elsewhere, because I hate being railroaded by fashion. And 2, any development, however worthy, is always pounced on by a thousand hopeless wannabes. For every Lonnie there were a thousand shit skiffle groups, for every Hendrix there are a thousand wankers with Strats, stacks and wah-wah pedals and I never wanted to be a bandwagon jumper. All the people I admired were one-offs, originals, and while I was inspired by them and sought to emulate them to some extent I never wanted to bask in some thrice-removed reflected glory. Surely the message of a one-off original is 'be yourself'. Isn't it?

NB: I realise I'm stepping on toes here, as one of the few growth industries in Britain recently has been in 'tribute' acts, but I'm not bothered about it because the whole concept of tribute acts is mental. Paying good money to buy a ticket to see people you don't know from Adam just because they're calling themselves Zed Leppelin or Fuck's Bizz is one step away from scalding your feet because the instructions said 'pierce can and stand in boiling water for ten minutes'. If you want to hear Led Zeppelin or Buck's Fizz, listen to Led Zeppelin or Buck's Fizz – if you want to see people you don't know from Adam, see them for free in a pub. For more information, see my book 'How to Eat Beans and Remain Injury Free' available from all good psychiatrists.

I spent a couple of months at the Crom then set out on a variety of gigs and sessions including a little trio with former Willie compatriot Roger Sutton on bass and future Rubette drummer John Richardson. We rehearsed at Rog's house during the day and did the odd gig when Rog wasn't working with his 'big boy's' band The Brian Auger Trinity, and that's how I first heard about Jimi Hendrix.

He'd jammed with the Trinity on, I think, his first or second night in England and Rog was full of it the next day. He didn't know who Hendrix was then, just 'some black guy Chas Chandler brought in' but he had blown everybody away, Rog said, including the likes of Eric Clapton who was in the audience that night. Word spread like wildfire, and the next thing I knew I was listening to 'Purple Haze' and wondering what planet this guy came from. For my money there are three guitar players who transcend even the best of the rest. Django and Wes are two of them. Hendrix is the third.

1968 was notable for several things, most notably for me the release of Hendrix's 'Electric Ladyland' and the marriage of Anthony John Thorpe and Shirley Atherton at Chipping Ongar in Essex, with Margaret Robinson as chief bridesmaid, Roger Sutton as best man and Rev Loveland (as in 'in love land with me and my girl') presiding. The bride walked down the aisle to the tune of… well, we weren't sure what tune it was but it was supposed to be 'Here Comes the Bride', and with Alf Garnett being the king of TV comedy at the time, the best laugh came when the priest said 'till death us do part'. The reception was in Tottenham, and I supplied the band because I didn't trust anyone else to do it. There was no honeymoon because the happy couple were skint. Here's Diane with the weather.

I know you're not supposed to say this... that's a point, *why* aren't you supposed to say it? I've no idea. Anyway, I know you're not supposed to, but as well as being head over heels/ elbow over ankle and bluebirds over the white cliffs of Dover in love with Shirle she drove me absolutely nuts in the birds and bees department. I simply couldn't get enough of her, and when I was getting enough of her the feelings were overwhelming. I honestly didn't look at another woman for years once I'd met her, and when I did it just made me think of her. God, I must have been a bloody pest. Some women complain that their blokes don't kiss and cuddle them enough, or if they do they're 'after something'. But that's not fair. I was delighted to have a kiss and cuddle with Shirle, but whenever I did she set every fibre of my sexual being alight and you can't just leave a bloke burning or he'll char the furniture. Here's Diane with the weather.

NB: You may notice in this tome that I never mention holidays, and there's a reason for that. Shirle and I only ever had two – a week in Malta, because I'd been there with Willie and loved it (especially the buses, which the drivers decorated themselves, and always with pictures of Elvis and Jesus, how fab is that) and a week in North Wales ten years later, paid for by a charity. If I've had the time I didn't have the money, and if I've had the money I didn't have the time. Just thought I'd mention it.

The Pits…

For the next few months I got by with the occasional session and some gigs with a country band, but this was freelance work with the accent on the 'free' and Shirle was beginning to get the hump bringing home the bacon selling spuds in my parents' shop, so I put out some feelers (they can't touch you for it) and up came the chance of a pit gig at a summer season in Great Yarmouth, a rather daunting prospect as I'd never played with a full orchestra before, I hadn't read any dots since 'The Way You Look Tonight' arranged by Jimmy Lally in Eb, and this was a pro outfit. One of the best, by all accounts, the Coventry Theatre Orchestra. Still, faint heart never won a summer season in Great Yarmouth with the Coventry Theatre Orchestra, so I packed my guitar, amp and Shirle into the car and pointed it at Norfolk. It turned out to be a fucking great move.

Arriving in Yarmouth a day early, we found ourselves somewhere to stay – a little caravan on quite a large caravan site. (The following year we saw on the TV news that this caravan, along with at least half the others on the site, had been caught in a flood and ended up in the North Sea). The next day I presented myself at the theatre for rehearsals to find sixteen seasoned readers and their Musical Director. I shit myself, introduced myself and quickly scanned the guitar 'book' - almost all chords with just a few bars of top line. I unshit myself immediately.

Following the MD's stick was a new experience but by tea break I was feeling positive, and while the others took their break I ran over the few bits of top line and I was set. The band had clearly earned its reputation because it mastered the music quickly and felt and sounded wonderful, one of the main reasons being one of the other best bosses I ever had, their MD Bill Pethers.

Bill was in his seventies by then and he'd worked with just about everybody. He had even worked with Laurel & Hardy when they came to Britain, and as a result knew everything there was to know about leading a great theatre band. But Bill was also a delightful bloke and a great man-manager, which meant that his musicians loved him as a man as much as they respected him as a musician and you can't get better than that.

The icing on this cake was Bill's right-hand man, pianist Peter Collins, because as well as being one of the sweetest, gentlest men I've ever known, he knew everything there was to know about music and I tried to ensure he passed as much as possible over to me. This kind of opportunity is sadly lacking today, when most rock and pop bands consist of blokes who have only ever played with each other. They might make decent records, one of them may be able to write hit songs, but they're severely limited purely from lack of background, and if that sounds old-fartish I don't care. It's true, so bollocks!

The star of that summer season was Jimmy Tarbuck, who now has a reputation as a mainstream comic but was in fact more like the vanguard of what came to be known as 'alternative comedy', with a personality that registered on the

Richter scale, an attack that would have deterred a Panzer division and a line in ascerbic put-downs you wouldn't want to be on the wrong end of. I did a few one-nighters with him when the season ended, and finding the audience at one country club a trifle snotty I warned him 'they're a bit stuck-up in here tonight, Jim'. Without missing a beat he replied 'we'll soon put a fucking stop to that!' He did too.

At the start of the season Jim's act consisted of twenty minutes of gags, a spoof song medley, then five minutes of comic banter with Bill, something they'd apparently started doing during the previous panto season. This involved Jim pretending to be exasperated by Bill's advanced age – 'silly old fool, seen more hair on a piece of bacon' etc - while Bill played along by pretending to be a bumbling old man and half deaf to boot, as in…

JIM

I was just saying to the audience, we've had some very warm weather.

BILL

Yes, we're all together, yes.

It sounded funnier than it looks because Bill turned out to be as good a comedian as he was an MD, with a level of timing and performance most comics can only dream of, and Jim never came up with a new 'deaf' line that Bill couldn't improvise a great reply for. In fact he was so good that by the end of the run Jim had changed his act to five minutes of gags, the medley, then twenty minutes of the Tarbuck & Pethers show.

Jim liked to push this idea as far as it would go, and one night he hit the jackpot. The script was that every time Jim tried to tell the 'chihuahua' joke Bill would tap his music stand and shake his head, indicating that Jim was not allowed to do that gag. The deaf/silly old fool banter would start, and eventually Jim would tell the joke, which always got a better response than it would have done if he'd just told it in the first place.

NB: The joke runs thus – a woman buys a pedigree Chihuahua, but finds it has two hairs under its nose which shouldn't be there. So she goes to a chemist's and asks for some hair remover. The salesman tells her to spread it under her arms and leave it for five minutes. The woman says 'oh, it's not for under my arms, it's for my Chihuahua'. To which the salesman replies 'well, in that case, same instructions but don't ride your bike for two weeks'.

Anyway, one night towards the end of the season Jim kept starting the gag and Bill kept protesting, until Jim asked what was wrong and Bill said 'you can't tell that joke'. At which point Jim handed the microphone to Bill, said 'well *you* tell it then' and sat on the edge of the stage while Bill, God love him, turned to the audience and told the Chihuahua gag - at least as well as Jim would himself.

Jim loved this double act so much that when, soon afterwards, he was invited to take part in TV's 'Sunday Night at the London Palladium' he took Bill with him. It went splendidly until the medley, at which point it all went tits up and I was one of about six people in England who knew why. The first song was in the key of C, and the lead-in was one guitar chord, written on the guitar part as a G major. I instinctively knew that to lead him into the key of C Jim would need a G^7 or, better still, a G^7augmented, which was what I'd always given him. Instead of which the guitarist at the Palladium played exactly what was written, propelling Jim into the key of G and causing the whole thing to fall apart. *On live television*. This is a perfect example of why ears and understanding are more important than reading skills, a topic I shall refer to again in this piece. You have been warned.

As with every other theatre show I ever did, I found Jim and the other 'principles' in his summer season delightful, but from what I heard this wasn't always the case and theatre musicians were not slow to wreak their revenge on arrogant or unpleasant stars. The favourite trick, I was told, was to add a sharp or two (or flat or two) to the victim's band parts, each member of the orchestra adding as many or few as he wanted and thus rendering the music unplayable at the performer's next gig. Cheeky, that. But in one case (I'll mention no names) this punishment was considered too mild to fit the crime, so as well as altering the key signatures the band put half his music in a case going to his next gig and the other half in a box going straight to Finland. *Expensive*, that.

Where was I? Oh, yeah, I got on well with everybody on that season and I was sorry when it ended. Shirle wasn't so sorry as she'd spent every night on her own in the caravan and when she went to pack her clothes to go home she found the damp had turned everything green. Still, at least she didn't drown.

NB: I saw another example of Tarbuck's attacking put-downs when I played Wakefield Theatre Club with him. He was ten minutes into his act when he spotted a bloke tucking into steak and chips at the table in front of the stage and asked, politely, 'how's the grub'? The bloke glared at him. 'I'm eating' he barked, 'get on with your work'. Well... Jim spent the next ten minutes taking this bloke apart bit by bit until there was nothing left but the skin on his teeth, while the rest of the audience responded by yelling 'give it to him, Jim, he's like this every week, the miserable bastard'! It was a fantastic example of how to deal with one man's rudeness and win everybody else over at the same time. I wish I could do that.

I was asked back by Bill for that year's panto, 'Humpty Dumpty' with Jimmy Clitheroe and Mike Yarwood, this time at the Coventry Theatre itself. It wasn't as much fun as the summer season had been, but the theatre was magnificent and I said as much to Bill. He told me that the old theatre had been bombed during the war, and when its owners came to rebuild it they approached their in-house staff for advice. They asked the stage manager what sort of stage they should have, they asked the front-of-house manager for his advice, and they asked Bill about the pit.

'I told them to make it big enough to hold sixty musicians' said Bill, 'because although we only had an eighteen-piece band I thought the English National Opera or Ballet might want to tour and we should be able to accommodate them. They took all the advice on board and that's why we've got a great theatre. These days' he went on 'they'd probably just get a firm of consultants to do it' and he threw me a 'you know what that would mean' sort of look which I knowingly caught. When did we stop asking the experts we've already got and start paying outsiders whose only expertise is in talking people into giving them money?

As well as playing in a great theatre with an ample pit I got to play drums with the band for four nights when our drummer, Terry, went down with tonsillitis. I hadn't realised how ill he was, nor was I aware that Bill had been frantically trying to try to find a replacement until somebody told him I played drums too. He was desperate when he found me in the artists' bar and asked me if I'd do the gig, and of course I said yes.

I knew every stroke of the drum pad by then, having watched Terry do it every night for a month, so playing the parts was no problem and for the next four nights I had the time of my life. OK, it was only panto music, but if you've never played drums with a big band (and I'm guessing you probably haven't) I have to tell you it's FANTASTIC!

When Terry came back to work Bill took me to one side and said 'make sure the guitar's loud tonight'. I asked him why, and he told me how a trombone player had once helped out a band by depping for a bass player for a few nights, and how the manager of the place had noticed it. 'I thought we had three trombones' he said to the bandleader, who explained what had happened. 'Hmmm' said the manager, 'well it sounds fine with two trombones, tell him not to bother coming back'. As they say, no good deed ever goes unpunished.

The panto breezed along fine until the day of the big snow. I'd taken the car into a garage in the morning for a wee repair (can't remember what) and agreed to pick it up later, but it started snowing at noon and by four o'clock nothing in Coventry was moving. As luck would have it our flat was only a mile or so from the theatre so I decided to walk it, and when I looked down on the town centre I couldn't believe it – the big roundabout at the bottom of the hill was ringed by static traffic, with roads of standing cars radiating out from it like a Lowry painting.

When I got to the theatre I found that all the principles had arrived but only three of the band (including me) and we started the show with an audience of about twelve and a band consisting of piano, alto sax and guitar. From then on it was more entertaining watching the pit and the front-of-house than watching the show, as audience members and frazzled musicians appeared one by one while the show progressed on stage. A bookie could have had a field day taking bets on who would arrive next and which would fill up first, the pit, the stalls, the balcony or the upper circle, and we didn't get a full complement in any of them until the panto was twenty minutes from the end. Then everyone had to get home again. Showbiz, eh?

There's a sequel to this story too, because someone suggested the theatre put on a special matinee performance to reward all the city's paper boys and girls for braving the snow to deliver the papers, and there were a lot of paper boys and girls. Unfortunately whoever organised the event only sent about four adults to supervise a couple of thousand kids, and none of them were armed. Big mistake.

Kids in the upper circle were dropping food, drinks, opera glasses and lighted cigarettes onto the kids in the balcony, who were doing likewise to the kids in the stalls. But, more lethally, some were throwing coins towards the stage, most of which didn't quite reach. Now I didn't know this, but a coin thrown from the upper circle of the Coventry Theatre was quite capable of cracking a Zildjian cymbal, a drum skin or a human skull, and would go through a 300-year-old violin like a knife through butter. And as we had a few of those you can imagine the panic.

Naturally the theatre manager stopped the show a few times to appeal for order, but where unsupervised kids are concerned that's like appealing for calm to a stampeding herd of bison. We discussed mounting machine guns on the pit rail but all of ours were at the menders, so there was nothing we could do but keep going to the bitter end, just do it faster. There's a moral to this story – if anyone suggests you do a special show for kids, use the old anti-drugs line and 'just say NO'!

Following straight on from the panto was a week of the Gang Show, Ralph Reader's boy scout extravaganza which was staffed entirely by people of all shapes, sizes and ages in shorts and woggles. The only professionals in the building for the week's run were the band, and when the reviews came out the only people who got criticised were... I don't really need to finish this sentence, do I?

A few months' enforced 'freelance' work followed (there was no guitar required for the Spring show) then it was off for summer season again, this time with Cilla Black at the ABC Theatre, Blackpool. In case you're wondering she was sensational. Of course I was already familiar with a lot of her material having bought it or heard it on the radio. Shirle had even used a couple of her songs in her own act, so no problems there. But the rest of the show was no problem either because by then I had become a seasoned pit musician myself and we had a terrific run.

This time Shirle and I rented a gorgeous little flat rather than a caravan, but she didn't fancy sitting in that all season either, so she got herself a job as an usherette at the ABC. I only mention this because it took her no more than a month to get all the usherettes out on strike. She had found out (through me) that a cup of tea in the artists' bar cost less than the usherettes were paying out front, and she took exception to the fact that a star like Cilla Black was paying less for her tea than a poorly-paid usherette. Shirle won. When the season ended, Cilla asked me to go to Glasgow with her but I turned her down. I can't remember why exactly, maybe it was because I was a stupid bastard.

It was in the middle of that season that the American National Aeronautic & Space Administration (NASA), after much heated debate in both houses, decided to allow Apollo 11 land on the moon on my birthday. It was the least they could do, frankly, and I sat up until the early hours of the morning watching it on the TV in my underpants ('how the TV got in my underpants' etc…Groucho Marx, 1938) and getting slowly pissed. I was delighted when the Eagle landed, and according to Shirle kept her awake by repeating 'they did it on my birthday'! over and over again. Of course some people say the Americans didn't really land on the moon and that my birthday was actually mocked up in a warehouse somewhere, but I'm convinced the Russians would have tumbled that one. After all they sent me a lovely card.

NB: For all those who dream of a career based on hit records, here's a thought courtesy of our Cilla. She said the best day of her life was the day she realised it no longer mattered whether her next record was a hit or not. I'd never thought of it that way before, but of course it made immediate sense.

More 'freelance' things followed, but as luck would have it Cilla's next season was the Spring Show at the good old Coventry Theatre and I gladly stepped inside with her again there. Between Glasgow and Coventry she had released a new single, 'Surround Yourself with Sorrow', which had a couple of little guitar-and-bass breaks in it, and assuming she'd be putting it in the act I had ear'oled it and memorised them. Come the first rehearsal, up came the music for 'Surround Yourself' and when I saw those breaks written down I laughed; they sounded simple but they looked horrendous and sure enough Don the bass player, a reader, couldn't play them.

I suggested he forget the dots and play them by ear, but readers can't. They just can't. He mastered them eventually but it took a couple of days. Now here is the first lesson – use your ears. That is, after all, the way music goes in. Sorry if it's obvious. I have never been in a situation where my ears didn't get me out of trouble. Being able to read is fine, but if it's all you've got it's… well it's like not being able to hold a conversation unless someone else is writing all the words out for you. Got it? Good.

NB: Roger Sutton once told me he was backing a soul act in a club when he was handed a bass part that was almost entirely black with dots. Being soul music it was full of syncopated push-beats too, making it virtually unplayable, but ever the professional Rog started ploughing through it. It sounded familiar somehow, he said, and then it dawned on him: he had been the bass player on the original record, for which he'd been given a simple chord chart with 'play funk' written on it. Rog had improvised the bass part, someone had transcribed it note for note and that's what he had been handed in the club – his own bass line. That's the difference between real pros and the other sort; the real ones know that a few chords and 'play funk' are all it needs.

NB (again): I think it was around this time I got to see Stevie Wonder. All theatre seasons run six days a week, with something different coming for one-night 'Sunday Concerts', and when I heard that Stevie Wonder was coming I made sure I was there (perks of the job!) I settled down in my seat, the band came on and started playing and I spent the rest of the gig watching the bass player. He was incredible. I had no idea who he was then, but I realised years later it was James Jamerson, the father of funk bass playing and, for my money, still the best (which is often the case). One of my proudest achievements is that earlier in the day I had held the gents' toilet door open for him. Yes folks, I once held a toilet door open for James Jamerson, and if that ain't something to be proud of I don't know what is.

Back to the plot. A brief respite this time, then it was back to Blackpool with Tommy Steele. It struck me as a mite bizarre at the time that while I was listening to a lot of the latest music I often found myself playing or mixing with the people I'd been inspired by ten or fifteen years earlier and Tom was no exception. He'd had some huge hits, quite a few of which I'd bought, so it was a privilege for me to be working with him.

Tom's show differed from the last few I'd done in several ways. There were no support acts as such, the whole first half of the show was given over to the Young Generation while Tom did the entire second half himself, and I was far more personally involved with him than I had been with anyone since Willie. For starters the band (a bigger band than usual, with singers) was behind him on stage, not in the pit, and he would end the show with a set of rock 'n' roll stuff which involved me directly, both playing guitar and singing a bit of harmony. Consequently when I arrived at the theatre every night I would visit him in his dressing room where he kept two beautiful Martin acoustic guitars, one six-string, one twelve, and we would jam a little.

He surprised me quite a bit, Tommy did, because his stage persona is very precise and a little saccharine for my taste. Off stage, though, he was as natural and down-to-earth as you could get, a genuine Bermondsey boy, and I couldn't help asking him why he didn't show the real Tom on stage. His answer stunned me. He didn't have the confidence. The stage persona made him feel safe, he said, as did the meticulously-rehearsed show. And it was meticulous, believe me. Anyway, to cut a long story short, one night all the electrical equipment on the stage failed and Tom was obliged to go out on the catwalk and chat to the audience, ad-lib, until someone sorted it out. And guess what? It was awful... no, it was terrific and so was he. Mind you the regular show was terrific too. Of course it was. He was Tommy Steele. In fact I think he still is.

Tom once told me a great story about his early days, one of those stories that manages to be threatening and heart-warming at the same time. It runs thus. Round about the time he was filming 'The Tommy Steele Story' he got a week's booking at a theatre in Brighton, and went on stage on the first night to be greeted with a torrent of jeering, threats and missiles from the cream of the local thuggery who didn't take kindly to him being a star when they weren't. (This was not at all unusual in the 'good'old days – Willie always said he learned his stage craft from Les standing at the side of the stage shouting 'keep moving and they won't hit yer'!)

Anyway, as Brighton wasn't so far from London, Tom went home to Bermondsey after the show, and when his dad asked how it had gone Tom told him. 'I don't fancy that all week' he said, 'it's bloody frightening'. The following night, bloody frightened, Tom went on stage again in Brighton, but as he did so the doors around the auditorium opened and streams of hard-looking geezers filed in and lined the walls, staring at the audience, the clear message being 'Don't, alright'? It turned out that Tom's dad, who was not unknown within the Bermondsey underworld, had rounded up as many likely volunteers as he could find and booked coaches to take them to Brighton every night for the rest of the week to 'look after Tom'. Now *that's* unconditional love.

When the Blackpool season ended Tom asked me, our drummer Terry and Peter Collins to go with him to Las Vegas, with Pete promoted from piano player to MD. It was a fabulous offer and I turned him down. I've got a habit of doing that, I think. It sounds mental now and it probably sounded mental then, but I had never been to the States (still haven't) and I dreamed (still do) of seeing places like New Orleans, the Mississippi Delta, Memphis and Nashville, the birthplaces of the music I loved. Las Vegas? It just didn't cut it for me that my first trip to the land of the free should be to the land of the bloody expensive. Plus, I think, I was wary of ending up no more than someone's backing musician. I'd been someone's backing musician for a long time by then, and I wanted to try to get somewhere on my own.

So while the others pissed off to Vegas I threw all my energies into a band called Lockjaw, a great little outfit whose promising debut album was totally destroyed by a 'producer' who had no idea what he was doing. Now record production is an art few people excel at and we all make mistakes, which is nothing to be ashamed of as long as you admit it and are prepared to discuss it with the other people involved, but this bloke didn't and wasn't. He knew it all.

His main area of expertise was 'track leak' which he insisted must be eliminated at all costs. (Track leak, for those who don't know, is when the sound of one instrument - a guitar, say – can be heard leaking onto the track of another instrument like bass or piano). The only way to avoid this if the whole band is playing together is to arrange 'baffles' around each instrument, but then the musicians can neither hear or feel each other properly, and that was the case here.

We told him we couldn't play that way – we even took the baffles away when he went for lunch – but he had them put them back again and insisted they stayed, laying back with his cowboy-booted feet on the mixing desk and saying it would be fine when we got in some 'spade chicks'. What a fucking moron. Of course the album was never released, which was a shame because it really was a terrific little band. (Incidentally, track leak is no problem unless you are listening on equipment which allows you to isolate each track and listen to it separately, and who's doing that? Are you? I'm guessing not).

Recording is a fascinating business, though, and while I never had the horn (technical term referring to the original acoustic techniques, not... well, not), I've been lucky enough to see it from its earliest electronic beginnings, and it's been one of wins and losses. It started with one-track recording using tape and valves, which meant that everything in the studio – desk, recording machine, microphones, pre-amps and effects – was valve-powered, and the sound was captured on tape.

Because there was only one track there was no chance to overdub, so records were made 'live' in just a few takes, and usually very quickly. In fact the standard in the early days was a three-hour session, during which you were expected to complete four masters with hell to pay if you overran because 'time is money' moosh! Which meant you would turn up at the studio at, say, 10am, set up the gear, run the first song a couple of times for the producer to get the sound and then go for a take.

If the performance was OK you'd then go straight to the control room and listen back to the *finished record*. Abracadabra, magic! Ditto with the other three songs, and by 1pm you had two A sides and B sides done, dusted, and ready for mastering and release. All those classic 50s and early 60s records were made that way, including 'Move It!', 'Apache' and 'Shakin' All Over'. Even the Beatles' first album only took eleven hours. Oh how things were to change.

Les Paul invented multi-tracking over in the States, and soon we had two-track machines here too, which were used either to make stereophonic records or, just as often at first, to record the backing on one track and overdub the vocals on the other. Two-track went to four-track pretty quickly, and that was still the norm when the blessed St George Martin (another former alumnus of St Bastard's, incidentally) used two four-track machines linked together to produce the Beatles' 'Sgt Pepper' at Abbey Road. Eight-track came along soon, though, which was fab as it gave you a lot more options. Now you could set up, get sounds and spend more time playing and overdubbing, with mixing a simple matter at the end. It was the coming of 16-track that buggered it up.

Suddenly we were spending more time getting sounds, less time playing and more time mixing, so that the whole process became more industrial than musical with none of the old magic 'wow, a record!' feeling at the end of it. It also removed the necessity to be able to play well, so vital at first, because now you could do take after take of a vocal or guitar solo, even do a few and knit together a good one, like people used to do with Austin 7 cars.

Of course it allowed people like me to make entire records on their own, but the immediacy was lost and the finished records didn't sound any better either. I used about 36 tracks on a track called 'Ain't No Kinda Star', and when I compared it to Eddie Cochrane's 'Summertime Blues', which contained just acoustic guitar, bass, cardboard box and tambourine, his record sounded better – and fuller – than mine. Hmmm…

The valves went next, replaced by much cheaper and easier to maintain transistors, but where valves add harmonics and enrich the sound, transistors emasculate it. Digital recording, cheaper and easier again, saps even more warmth and presence, so that listening to a digital recording is like watching the sea through a plate-glass screen – you miss all the feel and dynamics. That's why people who can afford it, like Lenny Kravitz, still insist on recording to tape through valve equipment. It's better, simple as. And like it or not, vinyl records sound better than CDs too. If you don't believe me, listen to a 45 on a valve juke box and drown in your own drool.

I played a lot of sessions prior to the rise of the Rubettes, but I didn't enjoy them. I simply couldn't believe how little most session musicians cared about the music they were playing. They would play it well enough, naturally, but they took no interest at all in doing it or in the results of doing it, and I got the distinct impression that if I showed any involvement or enthusiasm at all I would be regarded as a wanker for doing it. I felt that I had to appear as uninterested as they were if I wanted to carry on, and I didn't want to be dragged down that road. The Tremolos' Chip Hawks made an album in Nashville, Tennessee, and he told me that the local session musicians took full and enthusiastic part in the playing and arranging of every track. Not so here, and so my session career never did lead anywhere.

This English preoccupation with remaining aloof doesn't stop with music, mange tout no. Our phobia of enthusiasm and enjoyment permeates everything, and our only famous ice swimmer, Lewis Gordon Pugh, illustrates the point perfectly. He has swum in both the Arctic and Antarctic oceans, something I would give my kingdom to do, and taken part in the Winter Swimming Championships in Finland, something I would give my kingdom to do, yet I've seen him interviewed twice and never once heard him admit he enjoys it. It's all about breaking records, apparently, and/or raising awareness of the effects of global warming.

These are both laudable enough, and he has indeed broken records in both the Arctic and Antarctic oceans, but indulge me for a moment and allow me to jump to a presumptuous conclusion – you don't swim with icebergs in sub-zero Arctic water unless you *love* it. It's just not the kind of thing you'd do on a whim, yet the English in him won't let him admit 'WOW, man, yeah it's fuckin' *amazing*'! Weird, the English, and it's about time somebody found a cure.

I thought I had for a moment back in 1969, because that, as if I need remind you, was the year of Woodstock. What do you mean, 'what's Woodstock'? Really you must put some effort in, you really must. Just as the idealist in me had hoped rock 'n' roll would deliver me from the days of old, so it hoped that Woodstock would be the start of something big, a full-scale re-evaluation of our social mores based on the concepts of anti-materialism, love and peace, the 'Dawning of the Age of Aquarius'. Again, it seemed possible at the time, in fact it almost felt inevitable.

We weren't there, obviously, but we went to see the movie and I was consumed by every aspect of it. The music was exceptional, the sound quality was terrific considering no one had ever mounted such a massive festival before or tried to record it, and ditto the film quality. In fact I've seen some recent music festivals on TV that didn't look or sound as good, and we've been at it for over forty years now.

But on top of all that was… well, everything else. The whole 'hippy' concept of freedom and inclusion, the idea of making love instead of war (always my own preference, given the option), the fact that five hundred thousand people spent four days together without a single one of them getting beaten up or arrested, the simple fact that no one had ever done anything like it before, I loved it and I would have loved to have been a part of it.

In fact it had a big impact on a lot of us at the time, and together with the whole Beatlemania thing it unleashed a tsunami of creativity the like of which we'd never seen before. It really did feel like a turning point, a new Eden, and for the first time in my life I felt a genuine sense of optimism. I should have known better, of course, but deep beneath my cynical exterior there's an optimist trying to get out.

Unfortunately he was given a severe kicking a few months after Woodstock when all hell (and some Hell's Angels) broke loose at Altamont. I'd hoped that Woodstock had been the start of something truly revolutionary (you may say I'm a dreamer, but I'm not the only one) but I was forced to accept that it was the brutality of Altamont that heralded in the new age and within a year the Beatles had split up, Cream had split up, Hendrix was dead, former hippies were making fortunes speculating on Wall Street and the cry was 'fuck love, make war and profits', which didn't have the same ring to it.

As it happens, it was shortly after Woodstock that I was asked to play in the national tour of the hippy rock musical 'Hair' at the Grand Theatre, Leeds, spiritual home of the hippy movement (no of course it wasn't, I just couldn't resist saying it). I was delighted to accept, naturally, and I can safely say it was one of the happiest months of my professional life.

'Hair' was a phenomenon when it opened because it re-wrote so much of the 'musical' rulebook. For a start there were no stars in it and it was so beautifully written it didn't miss them. There were two principle characters, but even these were interchangeable and the two leading actors would swap roles every week to keep them fresh. Other than that it was an ensemble piece.

The band – a rock band rather than an orchestra – played on a flat-bed truck on one side of the stage instead of in the pit, and the show contained a great deal of effing and blinding and one infamous nude scene. There was no 'curtain up' because the curtain was already up when the audience came in, and the cast of around thirty made their way to the stage by climbing over the seats from the back of the auditorium and/or swinging from the boxes around the sides. More significantly, perhaps, the music and lyrics were terrific – I'd bought the Broadway cast album, so when the call came I already knew every note of the score. All I had to do was sit on a little seat on the bonnet of the truck (the best seat in the house, as it happens), play the guitar and watch the show.

The nude scene, which involved everyone except the band, was at least five seconds long in dim lighting, so 'infamous' only because theatre censorship had just ended and allowed them to do it at all. This was the scene that closed the first half, and as the second half opened with two of the girls in tiny waistcoats with no bras they would slip these on before nipping into the artists' canteen for a coffee. 'Hair' was an amazing show, but the most amazing thing for me was how quickly I got used to drinking coffee opposite a girl with her tits hanging out. Honest.

The demise of Lockjaw left me a trifle depressed, but as luck would have it I was at home one day when I got a call from Tommy (I still swear I'm the only person in Chipping Ongar who ever got a call from Las Vegas) asking me if I would play his up-coming season at the Adelphi Theatre in London. Yes, Tom, I said, delighted, I said, and I recommended he get another former Willie colleague, Tony Bell, in on bass. Me, Tony and Shirle rented a flat in Hackney for the season so that we could do some writing and recording during the day, and as this was 1969 – Cream, Hendrix, peace, love and all that – there was plenty of that going on.

The first thing we did was to set about decorating the flat, and as this was the Swinging 60s we didn't mess about. The walls we painted black, then we got some polystyrene, cut out squares and circles, painted them bright orange and stuck them to the walls in as near as we could get to psychedelic patterns. We thought it looked pretty cool, but a friend of ours, Mickey Gower, topped us up by dividing his living room diagonally and adding huge painted cut-outs of machine cogs to walls and ceiling. We all did this sort of thing in the '60s and we all thought it was cool. To be honest, I still think it was cool and left to my own devices I'd probably still be doing it.

As this was a time before daytime TV we played records most of the day in our flat, which I also think is still a great idea. Not that I have anything against daytime TV – oh, wait a minute, yes I have. It's not that I think most of it is shit – oh, wait a minute, I do. Listening to Hendrix and the Beatles not only seems like a better idea, it was more inspiring than 'Location fucking Location Lofuckingcation' and 'Jeremy Kyle' and there wasn't an advert every ten minutes during 'Electric Ladyland' either. Call me old fashioned.

On the recording front, Shirle and I made a couple of records together under the names Jailhouse and Hamlett, we all got involved in some 'cover' albums for a bloke named Nat Kipner (John Richardson and Alan Williams were around for those too) and we all spent time at R G Jones studio doing Hendrix impressions and/or being psychedelic. Tom Brown, the singer from Lockjaw, was around, as was the sensational Moon Williams, it was a fine old time and full of ambitions that didn't come to anything with alarming regularity. We even went to a party and smoked some weed! I say 'some', Shirle and I smoked 'some', Tony Bell insisted it was fine if he smoked a whole joint by himself and when we got back to the flat he spent the whole night in the khazi.

NB: Shirle spent three hours of her 21st birthday in the khazi of a pub in Coventry because everyone in the show – all the band and all the principles – insisted on buying her a large scotch each. Bottoms up.

NB: (again): Someone once said that if you remembered the '60s you weren't there. Prick.

The Adelphi season was a blast – being on stage in the West End is a blast, period – and Tommy hired two Marshall stacks for Tony and me (stacks!? What were we thinking?) to ensure maximum oomph. When it ended we wanted to stay in the flat, so we got a gig playing two or three nights a week at the White Hart pub in Tottenham right next to Spurs football ground, with the occasional session with friends thrown in. Those were the days when you could rent a flat in Hackney with a couple of nights' work in a pub and for a while it worked out fine. Then all hell broke loose, on both fronts.

It started with a fight in the pub. I say 'fight', it made the average western movie bar brawl look like a warm welcome at a Buddhist retreat. I won't bore you with the details, suffice to say it involved everybody in the place and every stick of furniture and left the room looking like the aftermath of a bad night in Dresden. You have to say one thing for Tottenhamites, when they have a disagreement they don't fuck about. We went back to the pub once after that, then called it quits.

All hell part two happened shortly afterwards when our landlords at the flat, my uncle Arnold and his wife Babs, smashed their way in one morning screaming blue murder and various shades of other violent crimes for reasons we never did understand. I don't think it was Arnold's idea – truth is Babs was psychotic and usually pissed. In fact Ernie had once become incensed enough by her ravings to throw her physically out of a first-floor window and Ern, as we've seen, was pretty even-tempered. Anyway she was throwing our stuff about and foaming at the mouth at Shirle, and I was in no position to help as I was being restrained by Arnold who, as we know, was a mate of the Kray Twins. Long story short, we packed up and moved. To Burnley. It was Samuel Johnson who said 'when a man is tired of London he's tired of life', but Samuel Johnson never played the White Hart pub in Tottenham or rented a flat from my aunt Babs.

I never trusted retail. I hadn't trusted it since my dad put down the price of orange juice by a penny and the bloke three shops along put it down by twopence. The idea of deliberately fucking each other over contradicted with my sense of Christianity and struck me as bollocks at the same time, and suddenly I found myself working in an electrical retailers with a rip-off manager under the control of a cunt of an area manager. If money is the root of all evil (and there's no 'if' about it) retail is where they grow the cuttings.

This situation came about because, having moved to Burnley, the opportunities for session and gig work had disappeared, I had to make a living somehow and retail work was the most plentiful, but I hated the whole 'business' thing and still do. There's nothing wrong with having a shop, nothing wrong with being a shop assistant. It's 'sales' I don't want any part of because it's immoral by nature.

Businessmen say it themselves – 'there's no room for sentiment in business' they say, and they think that's fine. I don't. Have you ever noticed how only businessmen and gangsters call themselves 'businessmen'? For more information, see my book 'Men are From Mars, Women are From Venus and Businessmen are From Uranus' available from all good bankrupt bookshops.

I soon moved from the electrical shop to a TV rental store, but that had a cunt of an area manager too, which suggested to me that all retail establishments are ruled over by a cunt of an area manager and that, by definition, all area managers are cunts. I have never been disabused of this belief. After the love, peace and understanding of Coventry and the Adelphi it was like going from St Mary's to the hell of St Bastard's all over again.

You know, when things are tough all over I hear the cry 'any job is better than nothing'. I hear it from politicians trying to force their subjects to take any job they're offered or face the consequences. I even hear it from apparently intelligent people. But while I understand the financial imperative, what about the moral one? Suppose the job you're 'offered' is an immoral, unscrupulous or unethical job that treats other human beings as 'targets', is that 'better than nothing'? I'll give you my take on it here and now – whatever the circumstances, anyone who sees other people as 'targets' should be used as one. By the army.

127

Two interesting things happened in the early '70s – our money went decimal (which gave companies a golden opportunity to put prices up) and we started using finance companies (which gave companies a golden opportunity to put prices up and up and up and up and up). Yippee. The prices we all know about – what fascinates me is that none of the new money got a nickname.

Almost all the old coins had a nickname – sixpence was a tanner, a shilling was a bob, two-and-six was half a crown, five shillings was a dollar and so on. Now ask yourself, what's the nickname for 5p, 10p, 20p or 50p? Correct. Have we forgotten how to be creative? Are we all too middle-class now? Or is that the same question twice?

Do You Take Sugar, Baby…?

I either got the sack from the TV store or it closed down (or both) but either way I was out of work again and preparing to follow the yellow broke road to the labour exchange when I got a telegram. It was from John Richardson. It said 'something might be happening, come down'. As nothing was happening 'up' Shirle and I agreed that I should check it out so I took a coach to London on spec. Our John had become quite an in-demand session drummer since I'd seen him last, most notably on Carl Douglas's 'Kung Fu Fighting', and when we met up he told me that he had recently played on a track produced by Polydor Records to try to persuade TV talent show 'New Faces' winners Showaddywaddy to sign up to the label but that they had signed with Bell instead.

This left the track sitting around doing nothing, so John had suggested to Polydor that he put a band together to promote it and they had agreed. Hence the telegram. He played me the track. I didn't like it much but I kept my counsel. And so began the saga that became the Rubettes, a story of hit records, big successes, missed opportunities, friendships, hostilities and an education in the ways of the record business that no university could hope to provide. I'm not going to write a history of the band here as that's available elsewhere. I'll just tell it as I saw it from the inside-out. And there's only a few of us who can do that.

Starting with a finished track and nothing else presents an interesting challenge, like how do you create a look that ties in with the atmosphere and sound of the record? 'Sugar Baby

Love' was clearly a pastiche of the Diamonds' 'Little Darling' from the 1950s so we looked back to band uniforms and added some old Shadows steps. Wayne Bickerton (head of A & R at Polydor and co-writer of the song with Tony Waddington) suggested caps (as in Gene Vincent and the Bluecaps) and came up with the name (Diamonds/Rubies/Small Rubies/Rubettes) and I threw in Willie's old trick of the name on the back of the jackets. Voila! We had an image, but whether anyone would buy it was in the lap of the gods. (Unofficially we in the band later came to call ourselves the 'Rubbits' because that was the way the Germans pronounced it and it just sort of caught on).

Polydor released the record, Radio 1 started playing it and every week we would call to see how it was doing. The first week it was No 51. The second week it was No 51, and the third week it was No 51. And if that's not consistency I don't know what is. It seemed I wasn't the only one who didn't like it much. Meanwhile the various members of the band carried on with their various little gigs and sessions, and I filled in wherever I could.

It was on one of these gigs, a dep for Alan Williams at a cabaret club in Watford, that I heard, quite by chance, that Peter Collins had drowned on holiday in the South of France. He was 28 and I was devastated. Not long afterwards I heard that Tommy Steele's stage manager, Eddie Thornley, had been murdered by 'queer-baiters' as he walked across Wetsminster Bridge to see his mum. It was a strange time.

Then we did Top of the Pops. We weren't scheduled to – Sparks were, but their work permits hadn't come through and the Beeb needed a replacement fast. The first I knew about it was when I got a call, at home, telling me to get to Television Centre ASAP if not S-er. The others did likewise from various bits of London, and while they did that the secretaries at Polydor were sent out to buy the clothes we'd decided on but not bought.

We did a camera run-through at about 11am, which was a real thrill for all of us, but on leaving the studio we were confronted by a man from the Musicians Union who told us we could not mime to the record, as we had assumed, but must *re-record the track* in his presence and mime to that. I was gutted. As there was another camera run-though at 3pm, and we were nowhere near a studio, it seemed impossible. But somehow Polydor found us a studio, and the band was good enough to re-record 'Sugar Baby Love' in a couple of hours and be back at the Beeb in time to be fitted into the clothes and do the second camera run.

So we did the show, the record jumped to No 25 and we bet each other how high it would be the following week. I don't think anyone bet higher than about eight, and the rest of us thought that was being ridiculous. When the charts came out it was No 2. The following week it was No 1 and it stayed there for three or four weeks. Now if you've been paying attention you will have drawn the same conclusion I did – people didn't buy the record, they bought the image. And that's pop music for you.

When we went to Polydor to celebrate there were Rubette posters all over the walls and the desk in Wayne's office was creaking under the weight of Dom Perignon. I happened to drop in a few weeks later when our follow-up record, 'Tonight', had stalled at No 12. There was one bottle of Pomagne on a desk in the outer office and a single Rubette poster hanging diagonally from one corner. It may have been coincidence but it spoke volumes. They all said 'that's pop music for you'.

Doing Top of the Pops week after week was a new experience for all of us, and though we couldn't alter everything about our performance week after week we did make a different meal out of the talking bit in the song. For the first couple of appearances John just stood up at the drums, but after that we added something new every time – one week, a chaise longue for John to stretch out on while women fed him grapes; another week, two suited 'gangsters' who held him above their heads; another week, the fattest female model we could get (Fran Fullanwider, she called herself) for John to act it out to. I can't remember any more, but they'll all be on video somewhere at the BBC.

TOTP was a strange experience in many ways, but for me the oddest thing about it was the audience. The first time we walked onto the studio floor there were two or three other hit acts already in their places on the podiums yet the 'fans' were just standing around taking no apparent interest whatsoever. Only when the floor manager called 'action' did they rush to one of the podiums and start waving and whooping and jumping around, which struck me as quite bizarre.

They must have really wanted their tickets as there was a long waiting list to get them, and I assumed they'd be thrilled to see Paul McCartney or Abba in the flesh without anybody having to call 'action' or anything else, but I watched them week after week and it always looked the same to me. Now, I've never heard anybody else mention this strange anomaly, so either I'm quite delusional or exceptionally observant. The verdict is yours, but don't vote now as lines have closed and you might still be charged.

When you emerge from nowhere and have a No 1 record you are treated like God's gift, which is no bad feeling for a while. I had backed a lot of stars, now I was one (or a sixth of one) and I enjoyed it. For a while. It was like being the Beatles (for a while) but while the Beatles were a seasoned band with a wide repertoire and a vision long before they had a hit record we, by dint of circumstances, had no repertoire and no vision beyond one track, and if we wanted to carry on we had to come up with both. Fast.

Wayne and Tony came up with the follow-up single, we all collaborated on a debut album, and since the Rubettes hats were such a hit I suggested we include a push-out cardboard cap in the sleeve and call the album 'Wear it's 'At'. Everyone agreed it was a great sleeve design. When the album failed to sell, everyone said it was because of the crappy sleeve design.

It wasn't. The problem was that the Rubettes were too 'flavour of the month' too suddenly and had no identifiable centre. 'Wear it's 'At' was good but it was too bitty, like a collection of tracks by eight different people. This is no reflection on the musicianship of the band which was at least as good as any other around at the time and arguably better, but I'm sure it annoyed the music press because they started writing us off as a 'teeny-bop' band and helped scupper the record's chances. Bizarrely, these days bands of far less quality are hailed as gods by the same media that branded us worthless. Funny old world, init?

Good musicianship or not, we had no experience of headlining major concerts and consequently got a lot of things wrong. What had worked so well on TV didn't work on stage and the first British tour suffered as a result. Some of the European gigs were unplayable (stages too small, not enough electrical power etc) because the promoters hadn't read the riders in our contracts, and to make matters worse there was poison within the band – I won't go into details, but history shows it reduced the line-up from six to five, then to four, then to three and finally to two different bands who seemed to spend as much time in court as on the road.

First to leave was keyboardist Pete Arnesson, probably the best musician in the band. My favourite memory of him is seeing him order a dry Martini in a club in Germany and being served with three sweet Martinis. Pete called the waiter back, explained that he wanted one dry Martini and the waiter brought him another three sweet Martinis. Pete tried again, this time with sign language, but he still ended up with nine sweet Martinis, at which point he gave up and ordered a lager.

Pete quit the band quite early because he couldn't stand the nonsense that surrounded its image, and I knew exactly how he felt. We were all keen to ditch the hats, at least, as soon as possible and that led to some insane discussions. One I remember was during rehearsals for a kid's TV programme, where we argued for an hour or more over whether to wear the hats or not. I remarked afterwards that if we'd taped the conversation and listened to it back we'd have had each other sectioned under the mental health act. No one disagreed with me.

Pianist Bill Hurd quit next, and I've got a story to go with that too. He left as soon as we got back from a tour of Japan, and two days later we were in France for a TV show. There was a crowd of screaming, crying fans waiting as we arrived and one of them was obviously Bill mad because she made a dive at the car screaming 'Beel, beel…'. She leaned forward and peered through the window – no Bill. 'Where is Beel?' she said. John, always one with a reassuring word, said 'Bill est mort' (Bill's dead). The girl was horror-stricken for a moment, then she leaned forward again and screamed 'Meek, Meek…' and I thought 'well, that's pop music for you'.

Someone I must mention here is Doris, because I met her during my Rubette days and we've been together ever since. She's an Ibanez 2470 jazz guitar and our eyes met (well, my eyes and her inlays) across a crowded Ivor Mairants music shop in London, where I'd gone to check out flamenco guitars. I had actually been trying to acquire a Gibson or Guild jazzer for some time but I'd phoned around the music shops and no-one in London had one, so I popped into Ivor

Mairants, tried out some flamencos (Shirle had bought me a tasty little Alhambra and I wanted to see if guitars that cost ten times as much were ten times better – they weren't) and I was on my way out of the shop when I spotted Doris in the window and asked if I could try her. We fell in love (well I did) immediately and she turned out to be the best guitar in the world. I had kept a bit of turtle shell from my trip to Masirah with Willie and I stuck it on Doris's scratchplate. All this will mean nothing to you I'm sure, but it's my bloody book.

Two things that had nothing to do with music happened during my time with the Rubettes, quite different from each other but both extremely significant to me. The first was the birth of our son Clay, who came along almost exactly a year after Sugar Baby Love. The timing couldn't have been much worse because the Rubettes' schedule meant that I was hardly ever home, and when I was it was seldom for more than a few days. Which left Shirle virtually on her own with a new baby and all that that entails.

To make matters worse, Clay had been taken from her as soon as he was born and put in an incubator, and when she did get him home he hardly slept and stopped breathing a couple of times so that she was forced to call an ambulance. This meant that when I did arrive home after pop-starring all over the place I frequently walked into some severe, and well-warranted, post-natal depression which, to my everlasting regret, I didn't take as seriously as I should have.

There's a postscript to this story too, because within weeks of having Clay, Shirle was advised to have a hysterectomy. The doctors had found some 'suspicious cells', apparently, and as she was far too important to me to take any risks I was perfectly happy when she decided to go ahead with it. It seemed to go without a hitch, but when I visited her in hospital one day I found her in floods of tears and assumed the worst, whatever that was. No worries, she said, she'd just been watching a violinist on TV and it was her playing that had opened the floodgates. Really? Wow. So I bought her a couple of Kyung Wa Chung albums. I can thoroughly recommend her.

The other significant thing that happened was that we moved, on financial advice, to a gorgeous home in Essex which took the form of two 16th century cottages made into one. Nothing particularly significant about that, you may say, except that the place was haunted. (If you're still with me I'll take it that you didn't stop reading after my previous brush with the twilight zone). This, though, was nothing like Hornsey. It started with smells – fresh-baked bread, roasting beef, just-extinguished candles, all of which would stop as suddenly as they started. At the same time we met up again with an old friend from our Chipping Ongar days, Doug Mortlock, who told us he could 'see' a woman (he called her Martha) pouring ale into a flagon and that the house had been a stopping-off point for people travelling to the coast.

We neither accepted this nor pooh-poohed it. Why should we do either? Then one day I happened to be at home, heard a crash and walked into the kitchen to find Shirle wide-eyed and obviously shocked – she'd seen Martha, she said, and described her in detail. 'Don't say a word to Doug' I said, 'and the next time he comes round I'll ask him what Martha looks like'. The next time I saw Doug I asked him, nonchalantly, what Martha looked like, and he described exactly what Shirle had seen in the kitchen. Spooky.

NB: When Shirle told me she'd seen Martha she pointed to a spot near a window and said she could only see Martha from the waist up, as if she'd been looking over an invisible stable door. This meant nothing to either of us until about a year later, when we had that window replaced with a door to a new utility room and found an extremely old and worn wooden door step underneath it. It had clearly been a door to the house in a former life and had, probably, boasted a stable door.

That, though, was just the start of it. The house had three rooms downstairs, a dining room and two lounges, one small and cosy and the other much larger. This last room bothered Shirle; she couldn't sit in it for more than five minutes without feeling she had to get out of it. I, on the other hand, felt perfectly at home in it, and if anything slightly uncomfortable whenever we left the house to go shopping. These feelings were so vague, though, we made nothing of them.

This was all well before mobile phones, obviously, but every couple of days I would call from abroad to see how things were, and that's when I started hearing about nightly noises. Or more precisely, one noise – the sound of someone clomping in heavy boots from one side of the large lounge to the other and back again, and though the lounge was carpeted the sound, Shirle said, was unmistakeably boots on floorboards. And she wasn't the only one to hear it - friends staying over heard it too. So, the next time I came home I contacted Doug (he'd been right before after all) and he introduced me to a friend of his called Terry Edwards, a physicist and spiritualist who Doug said might be able to explain it. This next bit is going to sound a little Edgar Allen Poe but bear with me.

Terry, Doug and I went into the large lounge and sat there, silently, for about ten minutes. Then Terry spoke. 'I've been speaking with him' he said; 'His first words to me were 'are my little nightly jaunts bothering them''? This intrigued me, because if it was true it meant that 'he', whoever 'he' was, was aware of *us*. 'He's a rather unprepossessing-looking character' Terry continued, 'but harmless I think. He is afraid of monks for some reason, and he used to hide out here two or three hundred years ago. He felt safe here and was nervous of leaving the house. I've told him he must move on now and he will. But' he added, 'he may come back once just to take a last look at the place. Then he'll go for good'.

I was as non-plussed as you are. Was this all kosher? Or pure nonsense? I had a long chat with Terry afterwards and the last thing he seemed was deluded, but I reckoned the proof would be in the eating. Or not. The next evening Shirle and I sat in that lounge for twenty minutes or so. 'Do you notice anything different about this room?' I asked her. 'Yes' she said, 'he's gone'. Round one to Terry.

Back on the road I went and phoned home as usual. Nothing to report at first, then came the clincher. 'He came back last night' Shirle said, sounding pretty disturbed, 'in the *bedroom*. Every time I turned out the light I could feel him staring at me. Eventually I couldn't stand it any longer so I told him to FUCK OFF in no uncertain terms and the next thing I knew it was morning'. Everything Terry had said had come true - game, set and match to Terry, I think. The smells continued after that but our unprepossessing-looking friend never did. Now I wonder (and hope) if we did the right thing by him. I'll ask him when I see him.

I said two things that had nothing to do with music happened during this period, but one thing that did have to do with music was Clay. I saw him one day playing a drum along with a record I was running and keeping perfect time. I watched until it came to a drum-fill (one of the slow ones it's easy to foul up), and he not only played it perfectly, he played the silent beats in the air. I couldn't believe it. He was three, for God's sake. Clay grew up to be the best drummer I ever played with – not overly technical, but with a truly international feel and magic ears, all of it quite instinctive. Amazing. Truly amazing.

Although the Rubettes' itinerary took in most of Europe the one place we didn't get to see much of was my old ancestral homeland of Italy. So when I told my mum we were flying down to Roma for a TV show she told me to see if I could find any Cairas there. It was a bit of a long shot – Philip Marlowe couldn't have unearthed many Cairas in twenty-four hours – but I promised I'd give it a go.

So when we arrived at Leonardo Da Vinci airport and found ourselves waiting around for the rep from Polydor Italy to meet us I snuck off to a phone box and went through the telephone directory. No Cairas. Which seemed strange what with Rome being the capital city and all. So instead I looked up the name 'Cozzi', cousins of the Cairas, who had arrived in England with them, taken one look at it and decided to go on to the United States instead. No Cozzis either. Slightly puzzled, I made my way back to the band and waited for the Polydor Italy rep to arrive. He turned up ten minutes later and his name was… you've guessed it, Ronnie Thorpe. You couldn't make it up.

As with Willie, I made trips to what was then Eastern Europe with the Rubettes' but these were longer than the few hours I'd spent there with Will and, hence, more educational. The first thing we couldn't escape noticing was that we were obliged to take with us local 'tour managers', whose job it obviously was to steer us towards or away from what we were or weren't supposed to see and/or hear. They were also clearly meant to evesdrop on as much of our conversation as possible as you could actually *feel* them listening, though how much they could make out of five Londoners chatting in a mix of cockney and rhyming slang I've no idea. Maybe they were specially trained.

NB: This idea is not as absurd as it seems. I once spent half an hour chatting to a singer called Pete Lancaster in a German club before asking him what part of London he came from. He didn't come from London, he told me. In fact he'd never even been to England. He was German, born and bred, he said. He'd learned to talk cockney because he'd worked with a cockney band and they had taken the piss out of him so mercilessly he had learned to speak fluent cockney in self-defence. Language schools and colleges take note.

The other bands and acts we met in places like East Germany and Czechoslovakia were very cheerful about their social and political situation as long as one of our 'tour managers' was in earshot. When they weren't we got the real story, which I hope the dismantling of the wall has made a thing of the past. But there was one thing about these communist countries I found extremely positive - without the capitalist incentive we knew and loved in the west, their TV 'pop' shows were actually pretty good! Instead of the obvious unending parade of formulaic pop bands and teenage idols, their shows had jazz bands and folk groups too, which made such a change from the usual I think we were all rather impressed. Variety, whatever next?

Our strangest touring experience, though, was surely our trip to Japan. It didn't start well. John developed severe reactions to the pre-flight injections and was ill the whole way, the plane was ice-locked in Russia, and as we had been diverted from Moscow to a small provincial airport with no tourist facilities we were obliged to sit in it on the runway for hours. And to cap it all when we finally arrived in Tokyo we found the head had been snapped off Alan's Les Paul. On the first evening we were invited to dinner with a dozen Japanese business-types by the promoter of the tour, Misa Wattanabe, a very nice lady who unfortunately sounded exactly like our favourite Benny Hill comedy character and whose welcoming address rendered us helpless on the floor. We wanted to explain, but *how*?

Japan, for me, was like something from a Ray Bradbury story. They all wanted to be western and tried their utmost to do so, but they never managed to get it quite right. For instance our support band, the Mets (as in New York Mets) all wore leather jackets and blue jeans and sported rock 'n roll Pompadour hairstyles – fine so far – but on the back of the lead singer's jacket, in huge white letters, were the words 'rock 'n' roll is here to story'. See what I mean? Almost but not quite.

The tour got stranger, though, when we travelled from one end of Japan to the other on the famous 'bullet train' and spotted the same faces in the audience. The promoters had booked 'rent-a-crowd' for the whole tour, which meant that the Rubettes, the support band and the audience were all on the same train! This rendered the whole exercise pointless to us, and three of us were so pissed off by the whole thing that we paid £800 each to get home thirty-six hours earlier than intended. Shirle was not best pleased when I told her, but as they say in the joke 'you had to be there'.

NB: One interesting thing before I move on – we were looking around a large store in Tokyo and found ourselves in the technology section. Now the latest technology in those days was electronic calculators and this store had thousands of them, but I noticed that when any of the assistants did any calculations they did them on an abacus. All that technology and they were adding up with beads on a rack. It was just as accurate but quicker, apparently. Of course I bought one (an abacus, not a calculator). I never did learn to use it like they did, but I've never had to replace the battery! Winner.

We flew scheduled airline to Japan and back, obviously, but on shorter hauls we had already started to charter a ten-seater plane out of Biggin Hill. It sounds flash, I know, but it actually worked out cheaper than buying seven or eight regular air fares, allowed us to land at small airports closer to gigs and it meant we could come and go as we wanted rather than when the airlines chose. As gigs and TV shows usually went on after scheduled flights had stopped for the night it also meant we could fly home and avoid another night's hotel expenses.

It exposed an interesting lapse in German efficiency too, when we took the plane into Hamburg for a TV show. At that time the Bader-Meinhof Gang were No 1 in the German terrorist charts, and consequently we landed in Hamburg to find heavily armed police everywhere. We got through customs, did the TV show, then made our way back to the airport to fly home. There wasn't a soul around. We walked straight through the crew section, across the tarmac, onto the plane and off. We could have been carrying diamonds, drugs, bombs, AK47s, anything. We weren't, but nobody stopped and asked us. Apparently the security services assumed that terrorists only flew scheduled airlines, so when they clocked off for the night there was no need to cover the airports. They really should have realised that if a bunch of thick pop stars had thought of it…

Sometimes a great universal 'principle' jumps up and bites you in the bum, and one such came about when we were part of a French TV show which was filmed outdoors in the grounds of a beautiful old chateau. We filmed at night, the chateau spectacularly lit by huge coloured floodlights, a large marquee had been provided for make-up and wardrobe, and we shared top billing with David Essex, who had brought along his extremely attractive and classy young wife for company.

While we were waiting to be called to make-up, David got chatting to John Richardson and the two of them seemed to be getting on like a house on fire. Dave's wife, meanwhile, sat demurely by, saying nothing, until Dave was called to make-up, at which point she turned to John and said 'You like Dave, don't you'? John smiled. 'Yeah, he's a nice bloke' he said. 'He's a cunt' she said, quite matter-of-factly. It was a shock coming from such a sweet-looking girl, and an opinion I could not, and cannot, concur with. That's when it dawned on me – every man is a cunt as far as his wife is concerned. I call it the 'David Essex Principle'. It may not be true all the time and in every case, but I reckon it's a pretty accurate rule of thumb. Know what I mean, squire?

NB: When I was back on TOTP a few years later with the Firm it was Dave who made a point of coming over, shaking my hand and saying 'welcome back'. So, not such a cunt, then. But then we weren't married.

We made two movies with the Rubettes. I say 'made', we filmed appearances in two movies - 'Side by Side' and

145

'Never Too Young To Rock' - but I think we ended up in the cutting room bin in 'Side by Side' and our part in 'Never Too Young' was noticeable by its absence from that year's BAFTAs. Mind you, so was the film. I've never seen it all the way through, but despite starring Peter Denyer and Freddie Jones I'm guessing it would probably rank as the worst waste of celluloid since… well, since celluloid.

Our appearances included the big climax, where we mimed on a huge stage to the theme song alongside Mud and the Glitter Band, and a 'Sugar Baby Love' sequence in which we mimed to the track on the back of a flat-bed truck as it was driven around London. I must admit it was fun to do, but I've seen it since and it would drive Health and Safety insane. These days we'd either be bolted to the truck's superstructure with steel hawsers or edited in using CGI – back then we just danced on the back of a moving truck while somebody filmed it. Madness. And they weren't even in the film.

NB: Speaking of the Glitter Band, it's shocking sometimes how the mighty fall. I remember Gary Glitter (who wasn't in the film, by the way) when he was Paul Raven, and when he reinvented himself in the '70s he was one of the most enjoyable things on TOTP, always creative and always good for a laugh. You wouldn't 'wanna be in his gang' now, I'm guessing. The truly dumb part of the whole process, though, is that when Glitter was sentenced for his misdoings the Glitter Band's gigs were all cancelled, even though they'd had nothing to do with the man himself for years. Who said people were stupid? Oh, yes, I did.

I made my last two albums with the Rubettes – 'Sometime in Oldchurch' and 'Still Unwinding' - at Le Chateau, a residential studio in France. Best known, probably, as the 'Honky Chateau' of Elton John fame, it presented us with an ideal way to make records as there was no travelling involved, nor any distractions. We just ate, slept and worked for fourteen straight days, and because we didn't need to get home afterwards we would frequently record into the early hours of the morning.

For 'Oldchurch' our manager, Roy Farrant, suggested we do a few gigs in Belgium to warm the band up before heading to Le Chateau, which seemed like a good idea at the time but could easily have turned out to be the worst idea since someone said 'I tell you what, Buddy, why don't you take my seat on the plane?'

We were using two cars at the time, with me and Mick in his black Rolls Royce and the rest in the band's black Daimler, and we were travelling in convoy from Belgium to France on the autoroute when someone in a Mercedes cut Mick up. Mick, usually the most unflappable of men, saw red and chased the bloke, eventually waving him down to the side of the road, but as the Daimler pulled in behind us the Mercedes sped off again. Mick had calmed down by then, even saw the funny side of it, so without giving it another thought we set back off for Le Chateau.

Once or twice we passed a solitary gendarme standing on the central reservation waving cars over and as it was drizzling rain we complied, but it wasn't until gendarme No 3 that I told Mick 'this may sound crazy, but I think he was only waving at us'. Mick gave me a puzzled look. 'Why should he'? he said, and the next thing I knew there was a corrugated police van on our port beam and I was looking straight down the barrel of a machine gun. We pulled over, and two very young, very nervous-looking French policemen approached our car.

Mine, the one with the machine gun, said something, but it was mumbled and I don't speak French that well at the best of times. He said it again, whatever it was, and as he was pointing the machine gun at me and obviously shaking I told Mick 'I don't know what he's saying but I think we'd better get out of the car'. This we did, and before you could say 'Rubettes' we were all 'hands up' by a ditch with the machine gun pointing at our backs.

Roy, meanwhile, was running up and down waving photographs and shouting 'Rubettes'! like some escapee from a 19th century lunatic asylum. At first the young gendarmes would have none of it, but Roy's persistence paid off and eventually we heard mutterings of 'oh, c'est les Rubettes', the gendarmes' tension started to evaporate and ten minutes later we were in a French police station signing autographs and awaiting the arrival of a Polydor solicitor to sort the whole thing out.

Now, up to then I had been far too confused to feel nervous. It was only when it was explained to us that I realised how close we had come to le reaper grim. Apparently the bloke in the Mercedes had called the police and told them two black limousines *full of gangsters* had pulled him over and tried to rob him, in response to which the police had attempted to stop the cars while we – missing the point completely – had, to all intents and purposes, jumped three French 'road blocks'.

This had convinced the gendarmerie they were indeed dealing with villains, probably armed, hence the nervousness of the coppers. At which point I remembered reading about a bloke in New York who, being deaf and dumb, kept his name and address on a card in his inside pocket. For some reason he was stopped by the police, they asked for his name and address, he put his hand inside his coat to get the card and they shot him. It dawned on me that if one of us had done likewise… well, you know. I've often wondered what it felt like to get shot, but I think that's the nearest I ever got to finding out. All those dangerous places I'd been with Willie and I nearly got shot by the French, how ironic is that? Shame, really – it would have got us some fabulous publicity.

We had a little car trouble again not long afterwards, but this was a different kettle of fish entirely and this time someone did get hurt. We were on our way back from a gig, in Belgium I think, it was dark, and I was dozing in the back of the car when I felt it stop. We'd been waved down by a motorcyclist, and he was saying 'elle est morte' over and over again and pointing. We looked, but all we could see was a hatchback parked on a green verge at right angles to the road, with its headlights full on and an indicator flashing. It was an eerie sight in the stillness of the night, but the car appeared to be quite undamaged.

149

We walked back to it and peered inside and we could just about make out what looked like a couple of dummies, but it made no sense to us and we could still see no damage to the car. So we walked around to the other side of the car – it was almost entirely caved in and beside it was a small tree stripped bare of bark. Clearly it had come around the corner too fast, hit the tree side-on and spun to a standstill with its lights blazing and indicator flashing.

How long it had been there we couldn't tell, but when the ambulance arrived it was pretty clear that there were four people in the car and that all of them were dead. It was hard to grasp. They'd been out for the evening together and weren't going to get home again. I don't think any of us slept much that night, and no one said much at breakfast the next morning. The silent eeriness of the image was burnt into our minds and we couldn't help but think of the police knocking on the relatives' doors. No punch line.

People often ask me what it was like being with the Rubettes, and I always give them the same answer – it was like being at university 24 hours a day for four years, and that applies at least as much to recording as touring. I *loved* recording back then, especially as for the first time we were doing it for ourselves rather than somebody else. And we experimented, not as much as the Beatles had done, but enough to keep me amused.

Way back during the making of 'Wear It's 'At', on a Neil Sedaka-inspired song called 'Rumours', I'd multi-tracked all the harmony vocals myself, a trick I repeated later on

'Family Affair'. This was when Wayne was still producing us, and Wayne loved a bit of multi-tracking. There were often upwards of twenty voices on early Rubette records, multiple guitar overdubs and frequently two or three tracks of drums!

NB: I completely overdid the multi-track vocal trick on a solo album some years later, when I used my voice to create an entire thirty-voice choir. Fun? Not many.

Vocal backings were always a piece of cake, as everyone in the band understood the concept of pitching intervals. So having recorded the basic track, we just stood around the microphone, said 'I'll take the third' and 'OK, I'll do the fifth' etc and off we went. If we needed anything fancier or more complex I'd work parts out beforehand on the piano, but we executed those quickly too.

Lead vocals were usually straightforward too. Essentially, whoever wrote the song sang the lead vocal. The only time this presented a problem was during the recording of 'Baby I Know', which John had written and, as usual, sang. But this time it didn't work. No one could say why, it just wasn't working. So John asked me to try it, but that didn't work either. There seemed to be something about that song that defied the usual approach and it kept on defying it when Alan tried it.

It was thinking-cap time, so while Alan was trying I listened to it coming back in the control room, praying for inspiration. And suddenly I thought of Dolly Parton. Not like that (well, a bit like that) but suddenly I could hear her singing it, so I asked John if I could have another go at it, and this time I imagined our Dolly singing it in my ear while I was recording it and simply repeated her phrasing. I think it took one take. Sometimes – no, always – the best thing to do is stand back and listen before you go blundering in, and 'Baby I Know' is a prime example.

A little of the 'old days' came flooding back when we recorded a track called 'Play the Game' at Polydor's own studio in London, built and run by a geezer called Carlos Olms. For some reason we only ever used this studio to make demos, which was barking mad actually as it produced as good results as anywhere. Funny how you never see what's under your nose. So, we recorded 'Play the Game' as a demo, i.e. almost live, with the intention of doing it 'properly' at Lansdowne Studios later, but when we tried to recreate it we couldn't get the band track as good as the one we'd done at Polydor. Wayne then suggested we use the demo track instead and just re-do the lead vocal, but d'you know what? Course you do – I couldn't get it anywhere near as good as I'd got it the first time. So the demo of 'Play the Game' wound up on the finished album. And d'you know what? Course you do, it sounds as good as anything else on the album.

If we'd had any sense we should have realised that and done all our recordings at Polydor, but when you're in the eye of a hurricane you really can't see the wood for the trees. If I come up with any other shockingly trite clichés like that you have my permission to hunt me down and kill me. After all, we'd re-recorded 'Sugar Baby Love' for TOTP in a fraction of the time it took to record the original, and I think taking too much time over a track can actually hinder the results. Of course you have to be able to play and sing to work that way, but the Rubettes could.

NB: I once heard someone say that the White Stripes 'recorded their latest album on a shoe-string - £60,000'. Which made me think 'where the fuck do they buy their shoes'? There are people who take an inordinately long time to make records, certainly – Steely Dan, the Beatles and Frank Zappa spring to mind – but they're geniuses who *need* that amount of time to accomplish what they do. Most of us don't. Yet we'll burn up future royalties paying for it. Pillocks.

Now I have to be honest at this point and admit that I was almost always disappointed with the guitar solos I played on Rubette records. Good sideman I most certainly was, but back then I didn't understand the process of playing solos, and if I got a good start on one I had my fingers crossed all the way to the end. Yes I know, but I'm not going to point out the irony implicit in that metaphor. I'd read that a solo should 'tell a story' or 'take the listener on a journey' but I had no idea how to do it and as a result I was always nervous when recording one and, hence, hardly ever satisfied with the end product. (Exceptions are the solo on 'I Can Do It', which I played with a cigarette lighter, and my electric 12-string solo on 'Family Affair': if you can think of any more, TA!)

If that was true during recording it was doubly so 'live', so why the fuck did I do an extended 'solo' spot on gigs? Oh yes, I did it, and it must have sounded clueless because it was. The old 'all the rest of the band leave the stage' bit is almost always an iffy idea – in fact the only time I ever saw it work brilliantly was during a Count Basie concert when everybody fucked off to allow Sonny Payne to play one of the finest drum solos I've ever heard. In my case it was nuts, but I never suggested elbowing it. When I think about it now – now that I know what I'm doing – it fills me with shame. I mean, what was I thinking? Thank God people back then didn't have mobile phones.

I made a couple of guitar-related faux pas that had nothing to do with playing, too, both of them the result of sheer bloody ignorance. The first was when I spotted a Django-style guitar in a music shop in Paris and didn't even bother to try it because it said 'Selmer' on it. Now, I knew that Mario Maccaferri designed that sort of guitar and that Selmer, who had a huge shop in Charing Cross Road, used to import cheap European Fender and Gibson copies and put their name on them. So I assumed this guitar was a cheap copy. Only later did I learn that while Maccaferri designed the guitars, Selmer (which turned out to be a French instrument maker) made them, and that Django's guitar was itself made by the Selmer company. Which meant that the guitar I'd seen was the real deal. Now, that being the case the chances are I couldn't have afforded it anyway, but I didn't even ask. I can't be blamed for being ignorant, I know, but I still feel a bloody fool.

My second guitar cock-up came about after a Rubette concert one night, when we were taken to a night club to see the famous French romantic singer Sacha Distel. I'd heard of him, of course – he'd had a few successful records in England and been on telly quite a bit. But I was non-plussed when he started showing me a jazz guitar that had been specially made for him, to his own design, by the Gibson company in America. He could afford it, I didn't doubt that, but I couldn't understand why a romantic crooner would want a custom made jazz guitar or what he might do with it. Only later (he said again) did I discover that before he started singing he'd been voted the top jazz guitarist in France.

Like Nat King Cole before him, he'd been a highly-rated jazz musician until he had a much-publicised affair with Brigitte Bardot and was persuaded to make a record as a singer. The record had been a hit in France, and he'd been a successful singing star ever since. Now, why didn't I know that? Because nobody told me. And he, in fairness, didn't say anything about it either. But I say again, when I realised my mistake I didn't half feel a prat.

NB: I hadn't thought about this before, but if someone asked a musician how he would like his life to pan out 'I'd like to be voted top jazz guitarist, have an affair with Bridget Bardot and end up an enormously successful singer' would have to be a pretty fair answer.

Back to the plot. Although I was fully in control during all the Rubettes' early albums, I managed to have the beginnings of a full-scale nervous breakdown during the recording of 'Sometime in Oldchurch', which brought back a very particular memory of getting home from school, putting Lonnie Donegan's 'Lonesome Traveller' on the record player

155

and lying on the floor listening to it in the dark, because I found myself doing the same during 'Oldchurch'. Not to 'Lonesome Traveller', obviously, but I would take myself into one of the studio booths and lie on the floor in the dark during playbacks.

It didn't stop me finishing the album, but I found when I got home that hearing music, any music, started me shaking violently. I had to wean myself back slowly, starting with Mozart and Chopin, and it took weeks for it to wear off to the point that I could start working again. I couldn't hear the results when I listened to the album later, but Shirle swore that my distress was so obvious on 'Top of the World' that she couldn't bear to listen to it. That was her excuse anyway.

I had no such mental worries on 'Still Unwinding', but I did have a crippling back problem that put me in agony pretty much twenty-four hours a day for a fortnight. It felt like being perched on broken glass, and to make matters worse on the ferry trip home the sea was so rough I had to deal with the pain and watching people throw up all around me at the same time. One sometimes has to suffer for one's art, you know. To add insult to injury, I was booted out of the Rubettes soon afterwards and all my vocals replaced. Still, mustn't grumble, eh?

Of all the lessons I learned with the Rubettes the most drawn out and frustrating must be the curse of the live PA system. Frustrating because we never did get it right, and drawn out because we never did get it right. Whatever we did our own system seemed determined to shoot us in the foot, not because it didn't work – it worked fine – but because of its very existence. When I think how proud I was when I first saw it set up…

For starters, on huge stages it's impossible for musicians to hear each other's amps and without that it's impossible to get any kind of groove going, a bit like the troubles Lockjaw had with those baffles. In an effort to correct this you use on-stage and side-fill monitors, but however much time and money we invested in them they always proved inadequate.

We sort of put up with this as best we could until we were asked to play at a song festival in what was then Yugoslavia. Unfortunately we had just flown back from Scandinavia, and as the equipment was on its way back by road there was no way it could get to Belgrade in time, but we were told that if we submitted a list of the gear we needed the festival promoters would hire the same things for us to use on the night. Fair enough. So we sent off a detailed list of our backline amp and drum requirements and arrived in Belgrade to find they had ignored it and provided us with three Fender Twin Reverb amps instead.

Yes of course we moaned, it's what pop stars do, but it was too late to renege on the gig so we begrudged our way onto the stage and started playing, and about half way through the second number I looked at Mick, Mick looked at me and we both knew what we were thinking – this is great! We could hear each other perfectly, for the first time in ages. We were all buzzing with it when we came off, and decided then and there that when we got to the next gig we would scrap the old backline arrangement and set up as if we were in a club, with the amps close together and the drums off the riser and onto the floor.

The next gig turned out to be a huge sports arena somewhere, and we set the gear up as planned and tried a couple of numbers. Great, we said. 'OK'? said our manager. 'Great' we said. 'OK, Dave' said our manager, 'turn the PA on' and Dave turned on the PA, the sound filled the arena, rolled back over the stage and drowned us out.

The biggest problem with PAs, though, is that we never had a clue what we sounded like to the audience out front. Picture this scenario – bloke comes backstage and says 'the sound was a bit crap tonight'. We call our soundman to the dressing room and say 'Dave, what was the sound like out front'? Dave says 'fine'. We say 'this bloke says it was a bit crap'. Dave says 'no, it was fine' and we haven't got the slightest fucking clue who's right or wrong, which means we could have a great night on stage and sound shit out front and never know.

Any road, at a sound-check one afternoon I noticed Dave had left the desk (to take a leak, presumably) so I left the rest of the band playing and slipped off the stage to take a listen. It sounded horrible. I looked at the EQ on the desk and everything was set on 'middle' – the bass, the acoustic guitar, the high-hat, everything. Fuck it, it's my desk, I thought, and I re-set the EQ until it sounded better, to my ears at least, and when Dave came back I said 'Dave, that's how it's supposed to sound, surely'? Dave said 'ah, but it all changes when the people come in' and that was that. I mean, I suspected it was bullshit but how could I be sure? I wasn't out front when the people were in.

At that point I gave up and just made sure I could hear enough of my guitar and voice on stage and left it at that. To be honest, I've only ever heard two live gigs mixed well and one of those was the Eagles. Most so-called soundmen, if you ask me, can't tell a string quartet from a pneumatic drill and I won't have them near me if I can help it. Obviously in a huge place you've got no option, but bands these days mic everything up and take a soundman and mixing desk into a 15ft x 15ft pub, which is not only insane but self-defeating. I don't even use vocal monitors myself, on the grounds that if I can hear my voice coming back from the front cabs I know the audience can hear it. As for my guitar amp, leave it alone. I've got the guitar I want and the amp I want, I've got a 'sound', thanks, and I'd rather you left it be.

NB: Back when I was with Willie we both went to see Cliff and the Shadows at the Talk of the Town, formerly the London Hippodrome and probably the biggest night club in the capital. There was no sound man, no mixing desk and nothing was miked up. The Shadows used the same equipment they recorded with – a Gretsch drum kit, three Vox AC30s and Hank's Meazzi echo unit – Cliff used the house PA system and everything they played sounded like the record. If ever there was an object lesson…

NB (again): One day one of the Rubette's roadies, Long John, told me he was going to the Hammersmith Odeon at the weekend to see Don Williams, which surprised me as John was a proper rocker and Don Williams was a country singer. I asked him why he was going to see Don Williams and he told me that someone had given him the tickets and he wasn't about to waste them. Fair enough.

The next time I saw him I asked him how the Don Williams gig had gone. Great, he said, he had torn the place apart (that's showbiz talk for rapturous applause and cheering). 'It was weird, though' said John, 'because whenever I've been to the Hammersmith Odeon before the stage has always been filled with gear and this time it was empty'.

I queried this. John said 'Don Williams had an acoustic guitar, his guitarist and bass player had a little amp each and his drummer played a bass drum, hi-hat and congas. They were all grouped together front and centre and they used the house PA, so the rest of the stage was empty'. This meant that the whole band, gear and all, could have arrived at the gig in a station wagon. 'And they tore the place apart'? I said. John nodded. 'Then why are we carting twenty tons of gear around the world'? I asked. I still think it's a fucking good question.

NB: One of the delights of playing jazz (and there are many delights in playing jazz) is that the whole PA nonsense is consigned kit and caboodle to the great dustbin of Twat. Guitar, amp and I'm ready. You don't play too loud so you can hear everything perfectly, and the whole band could arrive at the gig in a station wagon. Assuming, of course, that you had a station wagon and a gig to go to in it. I have neither of those things, but that's another story.

Did I make a good pop star? No, not really. The 1970s felt like a massive anti-climax after the 60s. The break-up of the Beatles and Cream and the death of Jimi Hendrix left a void, it seemed, that was filled immediately with cheap, soulless (albeit commercial) music and I felt very little empathy with any of it. I wanted as much as anyone to make the Rubettes into something lasting, but the odds were against it and I acquired a reputation in the band as a bit of a miserable bastard, which I very often was. And, to be fair, I was no better looking than I'd ever been, which is kind of de rigueur for a pop star.

Truth is I'd have loved to have been a star – not a pop star, but the sort of star who could work the Palladium and get the occasional Royal Command. I've always loved real showbiz and admired its best performers, but I never had what it takes in any department to follow in their footsteps. I had skills, certainly, but I never had the voice, the looks or the charisma. If I'd been overflowing with self-assurance... but we've been down that road before.

Via the Rubettes, though, I did get to meet Hank Marvin. Twice – once when we bumped into the Shadows in Paris while we were playing the Olympia, and again at TOTP when I asked Hank about the twin-humbucker-loaded Strat he was using so I could steal the ideas for a guitar I was designing. Thanks, guv.

Was the Rubettes a good band? Most certainly it was, and a fabulous vocal harmony one. We used to do Neil Young's 'After the Gold Rush' acapella in our live act, and that sound always made the hairs stand up on the back of my neck. But there were too many internal and external pressures on what the band should be, most of them misguided. Blokes never came to see us and as a result we didn't sell albums, which is vital to any band's longevity. I knew this and said so. In fact I made a lot of professional observations over the years, but they were so often dismissed as 'another one of Tone's fucking theories' that it became something of a Rubettes catch-phrase.

We did start to turn things around eventually with our first gigs in England for three years, on one of which, I'm almost ashamed to say, we were supported by the man who'd inspired me so much all those years before, Joe Brown. The gig that sticks in my mind most, though, was in Glasgow. When the doors opened I watched the crowd come in, and they were clearly there to take the piss. We went on, playing stuff from our later, more 'mature' albums, and an hour later we had completely won them over. Fab, but within weeks I was asked to leave the Rubettes so I don't know what might have been.

I lost all sense of my own ability when I was with the Rubettes, so much so that by the time I left the band I had no idea whether I could play the guitar or not. Sounds ridiculous I know, but the lifestyle is so fake you can easily lose touch with reality. So I phoned Ike Isaacs and said 'if I come to your house will you tell me whether I can play or not?' Very nice man, Ike was. I went to his little house in Wembley and the first thing he did was show me a beautiful Dangelico guitar he'd just acquired, then he started playing it and I realised I couldn't play the guitar. In fact I felt like a musical cripple in front of him, because he had all that Joe Pass solo-style thing down.

I asked him if anyone had ever recorded him playing like that. He said no. 'I've made fourteen albums in my life' he said, 'all crap'. Don't make sense, do it? Ike told me that when any American guitarists were in town they would always drop in on him and they'd spend the day playing together, which explains a lot. Ike emigrated to Australia not long afterwards and I don't blame him.

OK, Tone, I hear you cry, before you leave the Rubettes forget the rock 'n' roll for a minute and tell us about the sex and drugs. Must I? OK, then, but you won't like it. For starters the only suspicious substances carried by the Rubettes were cigarettes and Southern Comfort, and they were both mine. As for the sex, there is nothing unpleasant about being screamed at by thousands of young women. For a while. Everyone should try it. For a while. But I never felt they were screaming at me; they were screaming at a band that was in the charts the way they always had, and when the band's not in the charts any more they stop screaming. Women don't scream at men, they scream at success. I have never understood this and never will.

Equally I am at a loss to explain why some of those women are prepared to have sex with the men in those bands, but I'm pretty certain it has nothing to do with sex. I'm sure that in some cases it's a sort of badge of honour ('I got Taco's autograph last night' – 'Really? I gave him a blowjob!' sort of thing), in others it may be a search for approval as they're not likely to get knocked back. Up, perhaps, but not back.

Most blokes, naturally, don't concern themselves with such speculation as the prospect of a threesome with a couple of nubile young women is every man's dream, especially if it happens every night with fresh women. But despite being as red-blooded as you can get without being arrested I eschewed such carnal delights. (See, I told you you wouldn't like it). Naturally part of me was tempted (I don't have to tell you which part) and it was hard (stop it) to do the old 'lonely hotel room' shuffle night after night, especially considering the alternatives (and it was impossible not to consider them) but God, in His infinite wisdom, gave men a get-out strategy for such occasions and I took full advantage of it.

Call me a wanker if you like, but it stopped me being an adulterer, kept me disease-free and ensured that no one ever knocked on my door claiming I was their father. The downside of this was that the only way for a socially-inept idiot like me to be certain of avoiding the advances of enthusiastic young women was to steer clear of them altogether, and that can be very isolating. I'm not even sure it didn't contribute to my increasing need for a constant supply of Southern Comfort.

You know, this 'screaming at stars' thing reminds me of another anomaly I've never understood and it's this. Given, say, a singer singing accompanied by a pianist, the singer gets all the applause while the pianist is just regarded as 'backing'. Now, the singer may or may not have worked hard at his or her singing. Some do, but for many it comes quite naturally – they just open their mouths and there it is. The pianist, conversely, will have had to put in years of concerted practice to master all the necessary harmonies and perfect his or her technique, yet he or she gets *less* respect for it, if any at all.

There's an old joke that runs thus. Q: what are the three most useless things in the world? A: The Pope's balls, a nun's tits and applause for the band' and you see it perfectly in things like the BBC's hugely successful 'Strictly Come Dancing' where everyone seems to matter except the band that's supplying the music that makes the whole thing work. Yes, Brucie gives them a wee acknowledgement every week, but in real terms it's about as useless as…

Only jazz bucks this trend (classical music apart) by respecting all performers equally, but I have to say that for my part it has honestly never occurred to me to regard fine musicians as nothing more than 'backing'. Am I weird? Don't answer that.

Touring with a band obviously involves long periods of travelling and/or hanging around in hotel rooms/transit lounges etc but I found a few things to keep my mind productively occupied. Alistair Cooke's 'America' had been the big TV documentary series of 1973, and with 1976 (Bicentennial Year) looming and the Rubettes touring many

American-dominated European cities there was a plethora of related books to consume, and I consumed most of them with relish (or ketchup if I could get it). English people love to take the piss out of American history – 'history? What history! Ha ha ha' – but it's totally free of the kings, queens, princes, dukes and earls nonsense that plagues English history and I loved it.

I became a Ripperologist, too, reading all the books I could find about London's most notorious folk villain and making deductions of my own. I even dragged Shirle around the remaining Ripper sites, though I think 'dragged' was probably the operative word. I'd read a lot of Sherlock Holmes when I was younger, so I tried to apply his philosophy of 'deductive reasoning' to the Whitechapel Murders, but too many years had gone by and anyway, if he hadn't been able to solve them what chance did I have?

The other thing that helped keep me sane on the road was Steely Dan. I'd first heard them over the PA when the Rubettes were browsing a clothes shop in Manchester, and I bought every album, taped them, and took them around the world with me. They were never huge with the public in the UK, but I hardly knew a musician or roadie that wasn't hooked on them and their influence can still be heard thirty-odd years later. They were the best at combining catchy pop songs with jazz chord structures and world-class musicianship and still are. In fact, apart from the Beatles they're the only band I can think of whose every album sounded like a 'greatest hits' compilation and if that ain't fab I don't know what is.

While the Rubettes supplied us all with a decent living for a few years we never did cash in on some of the things other bands take for granted. We never got free gear for agreeing to endorse it, merchandising was a recent development and apart from a few plastic watches and some T-shirts we didn't have any. For some reason no one ever tried to promote the band in America, which seems bizarre now, and none of us became 'celebrities' in the modern sense of the word because back then you had to have done something significant to be a celebrity rather than just live in a house with some other people or eat bugs. I suppose we made the best we could of it but I can't help thinking that if we behaved that way now we'd all be fired by Alan Sugar.

NB: Another spanner in the wealth-creating ointment was the Labour government of the mid '70s, which insisted on taking ninety-odd pence from every pound we earned in tax. You know, for a musician my timing can be lousy – if the Rubettes had been successful under Thatcher we might have got rich.

I'll end this chunk with a quick description of one of the most interesting 24 hours we ever had, if only to throw a spanner in the media's 'being a pop star is all brilliant and amazing' works. It happened on tour in the south of France during a blisteringly-hot summer, so hot that the previous night we'd all eschewed bedclothes and pyjamas. Fine, you might say, but as it happened our hotel was right next door to a cattle-shunting yard, and as cattle are like catnip to mosquitos we woke up in the morning looking like bubble-wrap and scratching like Victorian tramps.

Then we got a call from German TV asking if we could do a show that evening. In Germany. We can't, we said, we're in the South of France (told you) but the Germans said 'we'll fly you there and back in a Lear jet if you say yes'. This would still leave us perilously tight on time, but the promoter promised he would arrange for someone to meet us met at the airport when we got back and lead us to the gig, so we said 'OK'. I mean, a Lear jet, how millionaire is that?

Lear jets, in case you're wondering, are amazing. They take off vertically, you know, but fortunately don't land the same way. So 'woosh', off we went to Germany and 'woosh', back we came to the South of France, arriving with very little time to spare. We were met at the airport by our tour manager John Salter ('Sarge' to us) in our car and, driving a corrugated-iron van, a representative of the promoter, which would have been perfect if he'd had the faintest idea where the gig was. As it was he set off in the wrong direction, turned back and then compounding the felony by stopping for petrol.

Sarge was fuming, and when we finally made it to the gig (a huge tent in a field) he tore into the promoter so hard he made him cry. As there were no dressing rooms provided we were obliged to change in the back of our truck (not as unusual as you might think) and we were half-way though when our roadies appeared and we asked them the regulation question. 'Everything OK'? There wasn't always a happy answer to this question, and if anything this time it was worse.

They'd set up the gear on stage OK, they said, but when they'd asked the promoter's Algerian crew for a trestle table for the mixing desk they'd been flatly (and sharply) refused, not just once but over and over again. Eventually, given no option, they had taken one anyway, and been told by the Algerians that violent revenge for this heinous crime would be exacted on them after the gig.

Not knowing whether this threat was serious or not, we did the gig and set off immediately for the nearest hospital to get our bites attended to. (I think I'd got the worst of it apart from one of our roadies, whose knee had swollen so badly he was kept in overnight). We were on our way out again when we saw our truck coming the other way and flagged it down. 'My word' we said (or words to that effect) 'you've packed up quickly'. 'Have we got news for you' said our ashen-faced crew, 'as soon as you left we saw the Algerians coming for us with iron bars and Alsatian dogs, so we left the gear and ran'. Which meant, we assumed, that we now had no gear. Terrific. But what to do next?

There seemed little option but to return in convoy to the gig, see how the land lay and take our chances with the Algerians. At least we knew where the nearest hospital was. So, pausing only to write our wills we set off and almost immediately came across a four-vehicle police patrol. Who said there's no God?

Frantically we flagged it down, explained our predicament and begged for help, and the gendarmes, bless 'em, accompanied us (not on the piano) back to the gig, where we found all our gear miraculously intact. We also found a dozen murderous-looking Algerians wielding iron bars and dogs, but the cops kept them at bay while we mucked in to strike the gear and literally throw it onto the truck.

A few heartfelt 'mercis', then we made a swift strategic withdrawal, discussing all the way to our hotel how glamorous and delightful it was to be a band of touring pop stars and eagerly looking forward to the next night of unmitigated pleasure.

Ain't No Kinda Star...

The Tremelos were mates with the Rubettes. Alan Blakley produced our last two albums, Rick West joined us for them on guitar, banjo and pedal steel and it was Rick who introduced me to the music of Jerry Reed and inspired me to start laying down some tracks for a solo country project. I wrote and conceived the first few pieces while touring with the Rubettes, purely as a side-line thing, and laid them down in whatever spare time I had, playing all the instruments and doing all the vocals myself while Alan produced. I had completed about three tracks when I was dumped by the Rubettes, so 'Tone Control' became my primary focus and making that album really was a joy. It usually only involved me, Alan and the engineer of whichever studio we were using that day, and as I had the tracks fully formed in my mind before we started recording them I just spent the day yelling 'give me another track' and overdubbing instruments and vocals like a man possessed.

I had a single ('Girl') released around that time, and that got me some nice publicity (in country music magazines mainly) and a TV show of my own – BBC2's 'Sing Country' – for which I recruited some of my favourite musicians including bassist Roger Sutton and a man who would become much more important to me later, Grahame Lister, on guitar. I'm sure the Beeb will still have a copy of that show and I'd love to see it again now because I was so paralysed with nerves that I don't remember a thing about it. It must have been awful, though, because you can't perform in a state like that.

Nerves are for before a gig, not during it, so when I say I'd love to see it again…

As you will have gathered by now I had no intention in my post-Rubette phase of trading on my former pop status. I was no pop star. I was a guitar player, and where that was concerned I'd been in the wrong band. If I'd just left the Rolling Stones or Pink Floyd I might have been snapped up by Pink Floyd or the Rolling Stones, but no one was going to come running for an ex-Rubette, good bad or indifferent. In any case, I wanted to spread my musical wings, not cash in on some former glory. More than anything else I wanted to learn to play jazz, but I knew no jazz musicians to learn from or play with.

But… I did know a drummer who ran a little quartet that played functions and firms' dos and I knew they played mostly standards, so when he asked me if I fancied doing a few of them I bit his hand off. Not literally, obviously, that would have been ridiculous, but… standards! All night! I'll have some of that, squire.

So I did a few gigs with the quartet and found myself most enamoured of the pianist, Geoff, who always gave me the impression he was holding himself back a bit. Then one night we were playing a company dinner, the punters were eating and ignoring the band (as usual) and Geoff, clearly pissed off by it, took it upon himself to cock a deaf 'un to the rest of us and cut loose on a solo version of 'Tenderly'.

The result was jaw-dropping, a full Oscar Peterson-style tour-de-force of blistering runs, dissonant harmonies and spellbinding improvisation, full of power and passion and everything else you could want a solo piano thing to be full of and I was completely blown away by it. And it wasn't just me either - half the diners turned from their food to watch him, and when he finished they stood up and gave him a standing ovation, which ('applause for the band', remember?) is simply unheard of at a do like that. Staggering.

Now, as it happened I'd been trying to 'hear' my way around 'Tenderly' for days and failing miserably, so when we got to the next gig I collared Geoff. 'Geoff, what's the third chord of 'Tenderly'' I said, 'I can't hear it'. He played it for me on the piano and when he reached the third chord I said 'oh, it's an F#major 7th''. 'Is it?' said Geoff, which rather took me aback. 'What do you mean 'is it'' I said, 'you've just played it'. 'Yes' he said, 'but I don't know what it is'. I didn't know what he meant.

'What do you mean, you don't know what it is'? I said (see, I told you I didn't know what he meant). 'I don't know what *any* of it is' he said, 'I know what key I'm in and that's all'. I was dumbfounded. He could play like Oscar Peterson and he knew nothing, I mean *nothing,* about theory or harmony or chords... I mean, *nothing*? It made no sense, it was just miraculous, he must have had ears the size of solar systems, I mean how can you... you can tell how nonplussed I still am by the way I'm waffling. It was incomprehensible to me and yet it proved a massive point, because there are plenty of schooled musicians around who have PhDs in music theory and can't play a thing worth hearing. I shall return to this theme later.

Now, if you've been paying attention so far you may have noticed that I tend to remember things that taught me a lesson of some sort. It's the way my mind works, frankly, but then I believe that's what we're here for – to learn. Well, I learned another lesson about the same time, this time courtesy of my friend Geoff Sowden, who was then a self-employed insurance man but had once been the trombone player in the Freddie Randal band, a fab and famous traditional jazz outfit and, incidentally, the one that first inspired Lonnie Donegan to take up jazz himself.

Geoff, great player though he was, found it virtually impossible to make any sort of living playing the trombone and eventually went into insurance. But, having grown up with people who ended up running some of our major record companies, he got to insure many of their top stars for mucho dinero so he wasn't doing too badly. Anyway, he was about to stage a charity event at the nearby Hornchurch theatre and asked me to take part, an invitation I was happy to accept.

Many of his old trad jazz pals were taking part too, and early on in the proceedings I found myself in a dressing room talking to the wife of one of them, a trumpeter whose name I'm sorry to say I can't remember. He was, however, already on the way to being pissed and his wife, I don't know why, chose to explain the reason to me. I pass this information on to you now as a salutary lesson.

In his younger days this man had been so dedicated to jazz that he would flatly refuse any kind of work other than jazz. He would hang around Archer Street every day (back then it was the place to go to get musical work of any kind) but would refuse everything he was offered unless it was jazz, which left him often out of work as jazz was no more the path to glory and riches then than it is now.

However, the lack of money to pay bills became a constant source of friction between him and his wife, who was forever asking him what harm it would do to take a 'commercial' gig every now and then just to put food on the table. He was adamant, though – it had to be jazz or nothing. Then things went from bad to worse financially, and finally he reluctantly accepted a gig playing at a summer season in Torquay with, I think, Eric Delaney, and while he was there the 'trad boom' exploded.

Acker Bilk, Kenny Ball and Chris Barber all had huge hit records and every other decent trad band was signed up by record companies and given tours and broadcasts. By the time he got back from Torquay the boom was over and all the bands that were going to make it had made it. As a result, said his wife, he had spent the next twenty years working in a bank and had loathed and detested every second of it. And that, she said, was why he drank so much. I heard him play later and you could hear the heartbreak in every fucking note. Now if that ain't a salutary lesson in sticking to your guns no matter what I don't know what is. File it under 'missed boats'.

While 'Tone Control' was a joy to make it never did get released, which wasn't so joyful as it effectively left me with a £10,000 'demo'. 'Girl' wasn't any kind of hit and my follow-up ('Ain't no Kinda Star', hence the title of this section) sank without trace. The third single I released, at the behest of Al Blakley, was a disco thing. He knew I hated disco but it was popular, he said, and he asked me if I would write him one. So I wrote one, and when I played it to Al he said it was too good to give away and we should produce the record ourselves.

So we did the track, Alan found a singer for it (Clark Peters, who later played the villain in one of the best British movies ever, 'Mona Lisa', alongside Bob Hoskins and Michael Caine), added a couple of capable girl vocalists and started to hawk 'Boogie Airlines' by Desire around the record companies. He was ecstatic about the results – everybody wanted it, he said. He picked what he thought the most likely label, and on its initial release Tony Blackburn played it on Radio 1 and pronounced it the best record he'd heard in years and a guaranteed No 1. Yippee! A few days later the record company blocked its promotion and that was the end of that.

What?! I hear your strangled cry? My reaction exactly. It seemed that Boogie Airlines by Desire was the victim of some particularly nasty internal politics at the record company and it left me with another six grand demo. Not being a Rubette was costing me money, and with nothing coming in it was time for a rethink. We rethunk and moved back to Burnley.

It's not Barnet fair…

Having given you a brief outline of my hair problems way back when, I thought I'd break the narrative at this point to discuss the on-going saga of all things tonsorial as it's an issue for many blokes and both more important and funnier than most. And, as it affected me in different ways at different times in my life, it's simpler to just get it all out of the way now than keep dropping it into the conversation and making me sound obsessed. I'm not, by the way. Well, not really.

The term 'crowning glory' is pretty apposite where Barnet is concerned, I reckon, as a terrific bonce of Barnet really can set a chap apart from other chaps. Like the ability to pull or fight or fuck, it gives a bloke confidence in a way that writing poetry or having a good eye for hyacinths don't. Subconsciously, those things make a man feel 'like a man', and I'm speaking as an observer here rather than from personal experience.

It's no coincidence that major pop and film stars always had better-than-average Barnet. Look at Elvis's for a start, the perfect 'crowning glory' for a King if ever I saw one, and our Cliff's was as so close he might have been using one of Elvis's cast-offs. But there's more to Barnet than that because changing – and often challenging – styles have been a major part of music and showbiz since the war (I mentioned it once but I think I got away with it).

Even before the war it obviously mattered because three of the biggest stars in the world at the time - Bing Crosby, Frank

Sinatra and Fred Astaire - all wore toupees, or 'rugs' as they were known in the colonies. You couldn't really tell because they were good 'rugs', expensive 'rugs', not like the one that bloke in Tesco was wearing last week. Bad 'rugs' are so obvious they might as well have a neon sign on top saying 'RUG'. See, the rich win again, even in the 'rug' stakes. Bastards.

Après la guerre, though, Barnet really came into its own. The 'Pompadour' took off like a rocket in the States, with quiff at the front and 'duck's arse' at the rear (appropriately) and our Teddy Boys adopted and adapted it to go with their drape jackets, drainpipe pants and knuckle-dusters. The rest of the population was shocked, shocked they were, as the 'short back and sides' was regulation at the time, and when good old Willie had his hair dyed shocking pink some thought civilisation was over.

But… no sooner had people started to get used to the Pompadour when along came the Beatles with their hair combed *forwards*. I mean, *forwards*, what's going to become of us? And not just forwards but long – *long* back and sides. It's hard to credit the shock and outrage this produced from the Great British majority, and when the Stones turned up with hair even longer you could almost feel people exploding with rage.

Tony Bell and I, when we were with Willie, decided to test the water one day by buying bathing caps and hair-pieces, making our own long-hair wigs and going for a walk to see what happened. What happened was that a busload of schoolgirls spotted us and went berserk, screaming and clawing at the windows like St Trinian's girls on acid, and all because we had long hair.

Of course the hippie movement made the Stones' Barnets look like stubble, and before long Jimmy Saville was dying his hair tartan and red-white-and-blue and the whole Barnet thing became passé, never to regain its ability to shock and outrage. Aaaah. But here's the point, throughout all the various furores my own Barnet remained determinedly uncompliant. It was too limp to make a decent Pompadour, didn't like being combed forward after all that time, and when I tried to grow it long it flicked up at the ends so it looked like a 16-year-old receptionist's.

Then it started to go. I noticed it first with the Rubettes, and like all men I panicked. Bad enough I wasn't tall and handsome but I had at least been dark. Now I faced the prospect of not being any of them. Yes of course I tried stuff, rubbing it in and sprinkling it on, but we've come closer to inventing a workable time machine than a cure for baldness and deep down I knew it. So when a friend of mine suggested that shaving it off might produce a more striking image I was sort of ready for it.

It was the best move I ever made, Barnet-wise. Since dispensing with its services I've never had to worry about how it looks or what will happen if the wind blows, it's saved me a fortune in shampoo and hairdressers and I don't mourn its loss 'cause it was fucking hopeless when I had it. But... it did make me think again about wigs.

No I didn't. I could never have afforded a really good one to start with, and the fear of its being dislodged would have done for my nerves if I could. Rumour had it that Gary Glitter employed a bloke to sit on stage all night and kill all the electricity instantly if anything happened to his Irish, and I could never had stood that level of uncertainty. I mean, what would have happened if he'd been mobbed by fans? It don't bear thinking about.

But it made me realise that there must be a lot of syrups around that most of us don't know about. I mean, the 'balding' percentage hasn't changed – one in six, is it, or one in eight? Yet every band you see consists of hirsute blokes. In fact the 'rock' world is full of sixty-year-old blokes with eighteen-year-old hair. Well, I couldn't do that. The world is fake enough without my making it worse. But don't get the needle with me for saying it – I mean, keep your hair on, know what I mean?

Working for the Firm...

Why Burnley? It was real, I thought, and I was heartily sick of the fakery of the record business not to mention the part of Essex we'd been living in. I wanted to get back to basics again, and I thought my experience might be valued in Lancashire, respected even. How dumb can you be? I should have known that being a musician in England gets you no respect at all however able and experienced you might be. (When I started working as a local journalist many years later I got more respect from people in the first month than I had in the previous twenty-five years as a musician, and journalists, if you believe the polls, are one of the three most despised professional groups in England alongside lawyers and estate agents. Which can only mean that musicians are so despised they don't even rate a mention on the 'most despised' list. Thanks for that).

When we first arrived back in Burnley I was drinking a litre of Scotch a day, the legacy of my Southern Comfort period on the road. It wasn't a good idea. It shattered my nerves and turned me into a paranoid freak. Then Clay was diagnosed autistic and epileptic, which shattered my nerves and destroyed my spirit. I wasn't working either, which meant that within three years of leaving well-paid stardom I was an unemployed lush with a disabled child being treated like a leper because I had the audacity to ask the authorities for some financial assistance. I tried telling them I'd probably paid more tax in four years than some people pay in a lifetime but they weren't interested, and to make matters worse Clay's condition seemed to turn him into Damien from

181

The Omen. How my old woman coped I've no idea. I ended up in a psychiatric ward.

I only went in for a week as a voluntary patient but it gave me an insight I wouldn't want to repeat. I got the feeling that just being there meant I was regarded as incapable of making any decisions or drawing any conclusions for myself, which is a very unnerving feeling to have as it leaves you totally vulnerable. I did see a doctor but I'm sure it was only once, and when I did I got the impression that he thought I was nuts. This is all a bit vague because I was in pretty poor shape, but I know I told him I could only relate to the religions and the arts and that the material world made no sense to me, and I'm certain he told me I was wrong.

The rest of the time I was kept extremely sedated on what I think was 'drying out' medication, but it zonked me out so much it was difficult to write and I was trying to do as much of that as I could to get my thoughts into some sort of perspective. I countered this by surreptitiously dumping the medication, but doing it made me very nervous as I knew that if I was found out I'd be in no position to defend my actions because I was, in their eyes, mentally ill and hence not responsible. Shit, what a catch-22 situation to be in.

The worst experience I had in that ward, though, didn't directly affect me at all. I was sitting in the day room with a couple of other patients, one of whom was a young woman who was shaking quite badly, when a beaming middle-aged woman appeared at the door and announced to one and all that she had come for the last of her six electric shock treatments and asked if anyone else had had the same therapy. The young woman never raised her eyes from the floor. 'I have' she said, 'I've been having it for two years'.

The older woman smiled. 'Does it work'? she said, which I thought was a crazy question to ask given the situation. The young woman slowly looked up and eyed her. 'No' she said. The older woman's smile disappeared. And I didn't know which of them I felt most sorry for. Now I am in no position to criticise or praise the sort of treatment used in such places because every case is different and I'm no doctor, but it never worked for me. And the trouble with mental or emotional problems is that after a while, after a number of unsuccessful 'treatments', you start to feel incurable. And that, surprise surprise, makes you worse.

Shirle came to see me as often as she could during that week, and on one visit she told me that someone had suggested that a Baptist minister called Edith Glover might be able to help with Clay and that she was going to call her. I didn't know what kind of help she could give, nor did Shirle, but something told me I should meet her and I asked Shirle to sort it out for me. She did, and as soon as I was out of hospital she called at our house. We had a long talk, none of which I can recall now, and at the end of it she asked me how long it had been since I had read the Gospels. It had been a long time and I told her so. 'Start again' she said, 'start with John' and she gave me a copy which was ideally titled for an electric guitarist – it was called The Amplified New Testament. Now I don't know how she did it, but the words in that book hit me with a force I'd never experienced before and I quit drinking immediately and didn't touch booze for at least two years.

Clean now and feeling far more positive the next objective was to find some work, and in my attempt to get back in touch with real people I bought a four-track tape machine, recorded some backing tracks and set out to play the working men's clubs. A word of advice – don't. Working men's clubs are a minefield, with most mines unmarked and usually in the last places you'd look. The old performing adage 'maximum effect with minimum effort' doesn't work in a WMC, nor does anything remotely original. If you take your music seriously you'll be on your own, if you're any good they'll swear you're cheating and if you don't worship at the altar of bingo you'll be risking life and limb.

The bingo thing I could take, though it's hard to accept coming a poor second to a load of balls. The non-originality bit I took as a challenge (I actually got a request to repeat an original song in a working men's club once – I think it was the proudest moment of my life) but I've been thrown out of a club, more than once, because they swore I was miming, and if that don't piss you off I don't know what will. The music was too good, they said, I couldn't have been doing it myself. And if that's not a 'can't win' situation I don't know what is.

NB: Talking of bingo reminds me of the first time I ever went to Burnley. It was with Willie, and he'd been booked to play the Casino Club (now the Burnley Mechanics) for the week as usual. We arrived on the Sunday (as usual) to find the place packed with people (as usual). There were four acts on that night, and when act number three took to the stage we repaired to the dressing room to change. We then came out and stood by the bar to check things out and wait our turn.

Out came the bingo caller with his machine. He announced 'ladies and gentlemen, after your last game of bingo we'll have your top of your bill Wee Willie Harris!' As usual. So he started the game, and when he called 'two fat ladies 88' someone shouted 'house!' and everybody got up, put their coats on and went home. The same thing happened every night and we did the entire week for three waitresses and the manager. And I'm not making it up.

Around the same time I also got together with bassist Denis Wane and drummer Liam Barber to form Gas Company, a band that, in one form or another, would stay together for the next thirty years, and I managed to get a job at our local music store too, thus scraping together some sort of living. Clay's problems were further complicated when we were told he needed growth hormone injections (my job twice a day) and we seemed to spend at least one day a week taking him to some hospital or other. Then, to add insult to injury, I was sacked from the music shop for being 'too professional'. I can only presume they thought I was miming. God, however, moves in a mysterious way, and in a move that paralleled the 'John Richardson telegram' incident I almost immediately got a call from Grahame Lister.

Grahame was an alumnus of Sydney University, the sweetest bloke imaginable and a musician of prodigious talent. We had met him and his wife Cath when we lived in Essex and I was delighted to hear from him anyway, but it turned out that he had a project he wanted my involvement in. He had a song, he said, that he had co-written with John O'Connor about the lead character in the TV series 'Minder'.

It was called 'Arthur Daley, e's Alright' and they needed someone with a cockney accent and a decent sense of comic timing to sing it. They'd offered it to Chas & Dave and to George Cole (who played Arthur Daley in the TV series) but they had both turned it down and I was the next choice. I was extremely flattered. Well wouldn't you be? And so, fresh from the sack (again) I travelled down to London (again) and in the fullness of time found myself back on Top of the Pops (again), this time with the Firm.

If the Rubettes was a good band, the Firm was better and Grahame turned out to be a producer of fantastic ability. 'Arthur' may have been a novelty record but it was one of real quality and for the first time in my life I felt I'd done a job no one on earth could have improved upon. In everything else I'd ever done I could think of thousands of people who would have blown me out of the water – Elvis, Little Richard, Hendrix, Wes, Muddy Waters, Ray Charles, there's an endless list of people with talent I couldn't hope to emulate, but I could honestly say no one could have sung 'Arthur' better than I did and it was at that point that I started seriously questioning why I ever sung anything in a pseudo-American accent. We'd all been doing it for decades, of course, but suddenly it seemed ridiculous.

I thought about that and realised that English music pretty much ended with the Music Hall, because from 1919, when the Original Dixieland Jazz Band became the first jazz outfit to visit Britain, we dropped most of our own style and tried to be Americans too. A little bit of English music hung on through variety, most notably from George Formby and Gracie Fields, but when rock 'n' roll exploded it blew that apart as well, and since then we've all been singing their music their way, or as close to their way as we can get, and if you think about that for a moment you realise how dumb it is.

I realised it with a vengeance one night when I was singing Muddy Waters' 'Hoochie Coochie Man' with Gas Company at The Lamb in Preston and suddenly thought 'what the fuck am I doing? I'm a white bloke from Haringey, who the fuck is going to believe I'm the Hoochie Coochie Man'? The whole point of the blues is that it's sung in the same voice it's spoken in and tells stories its audience can identify with. Same with country music, and it used to be the same with Music Hall – British accents telling British stories to British audiences.

English blues singers? What the hell were we thinking? Can you imagine Muddy Waters or Frank Sinatra singing 'Arthur Daley He's Alright'? No of course you can't, it's ridiculous, and that's why 'Arthur' is the one thing I've done that nobody else on earth could have done better. English blues singers? What were we thinking? We don't even *get* 'the blues', we get pissed off! All together now, 'Every day, every day I get pissed off'.

Of course the exception proves the rule, and the exception in this case is called Peter Green. For some reason known only to God, the former East End butcher's boy could play and sing the blues like a native. Of Chicago, not Bethnal Green. For me, he's the only credible English bluesman and I can only sit back and wonder.

While I'm on this soapbox, who in this country calls his girlfriend 'baby'? No one does. Only the most extreme comedy sketch-show parody of the world's worst lounge-lizard would call anyone 'baby', so why does nearly every singer-songwriter in England write lyrics with the word 'baby' in them? Often over and over again? Hm? Eh? Yes, I'm asking you, why? Why do we do that? More to the point, why do so many English singers insist on pronouncing it 'bee-bear'? Hm? We're not only using a word we would never use, we're pronouncing it wrong. If your girlfriend or boyfriend was lying naked in front of you and you were just about to get very serious indeed and he or she said 'oh bee-bear' to you, wouldn't you suddenly have second thoughts? Now, write it out a thousand times and have it on my desk by tomorrow morning.

Any road, when 'Arthur' starting getting airplay, Grahame called me and asked if I'd handle any press attention as I'd had more experience in that area. I accepted, but said that the truth was too boring to create any kind of interest and asked him to give me a typical London-villain surname. 'Sykes' he said, which made perfect Dickensian sense. I turned to Shirle and asked her to give me a Christian name. 'Ronnie' she said, and I told Grahame that if any papers called he should give them my number and tell them to ask for Ronnie Sykes.

It was a hoot! Whenever the press called I would put Ron on the phone and 'he' would tell them how he had co-written 'Arthur' with Chiv Lister and Leather John O'Connor while they were doing a spot of bird together for petty in one of Her Majesty's hotels and the press printed it. I even did a BBC Newsbeat in character as Ron, and Grahame told me afterwards that people had bought the story hook, line and sinker, including some musicians who should have known better.

This kicks up an interesting dilemma because it suggests that people buy whatever they read in the papers, hear on the radio or see on TV, and while that doesn't matter in 'show-biz' terms it's more than a mite worrying generally. The Rubettes suffered from some serious misreporting once, when we were asked to play a major music festival in Paris and agreed to take an English reporter with us to cover it. We flew him out there, fed him, watered him and flew him back, and because French President Giscard Destaing's son had been in the audience his 'review' of the gig turned into a rant about whether English pop acts should be supporting European political parties. Tosser. I've since stopped reading so-called newspapers altogether. In fact I haven't read one in thirty years and I don't feel the slightest bit worse off for it.

Being back on TOTP with the Firm was tremendous fun, and to be singing lead vocal with a different band was strangely satisfying for a boy who had been told on more than one occasion that he was too ugly to be a pop star. We did a show called Number 73 with the Firm too, but I'd forgotten all about it until my great friend and bassist par excellence Greg Harper mentioned it a couple of years ago. I looked it up on YouTube and still couldn't remember doing it, which is not as unusual as it sounds; there are loads of Rubette TV clips on YouTube I don't remember doing either, but with the Rubettes these things just got lost in the torrent. The Firm was a different kettle of fish. Then I remembered why I'd forgotten it, if that makes any sense. It so happened that Gas Company had been offered two consecutive nights at a club in Earby, great news as it meant we could finish the gig on the Friday and leave all the gear on the stage so it was ready for the following night. Less work, see?

Then Grahame phoned me – could I do a TV show in Chatham, Kent, on the Saturday morning? I thought he was having a Steffi at first but no, serious. I told the chaps, and Denis, God love him, offered to come with me and share the driving. So we did the Friday night at Earby, got straight in the car, drove through the night, arrived in Chatham about 6.30am, did the show, got straight back in the car, drove back to Earby and got there just in time for the Saturday gig, by the end of which I was as creamed as I'd ever been in my life and that's why I forgot all about No 73. And I didn't even realise until I saw it on YouTube that the presenter was one of my heroes from The News Quiz, Sandi Toksvig. The Firm sang and played live on No 73, so if you want proof of the band's musical abilities check it out.

The pinnacle of the Firm saga for me, though, was when Dev Devlin and I sang 'London is the Biz' live on the Yorkshire TV quiz programme 3,2,1, hosted by Ted Rogers, who had once lent his dressing room to Willie during a chaotic charity show at the Victoria Palace. Two of the other guests on that week's show were Kenneth Connor and Wendy Richards, so we were in stellar showbiz company.

I can't explain this, but the only places I've ever felt at home were on a stage or in a dressing room. Notwithstanding the obvious semantic implications, I never felt at home at home, so spending two days of rehearsals and recording at Yorkshire TV was like... well, home. Our spot on 3,2,1 was also, and remains, the one and only time I was ever asked to sing live and move to camera direction at the same time, and I took to it like a Tory to banking.

Theatres and TV studios are the only truly professional places of entertainment in my experience, and their attitude of 'if you have a professional problem we'll understand and help' always made me feel totally safe and secure. As a result, the fact that 3,2,1 had a viewing figure of around fifteen million didn't bother me a bit. Put me in a little club or a pub and I'm nervous all night because I know they couldn't care less. Dev, incidentally, apart from being a damned fine guitar picker was, like me, a Goon fan and a whizz at doing all the voices, and I reckon we could have made more of the Firm if we'd treated it as a theatrical group rather than a band but at the time it didn't cross my mind. Idiot.

Speaking of Dev, we were chatting once during the break in a pub gig and I happened to tell him that when I was a kid I used to hone my independence skills by playing the chords of a song in one key and trying to sing it perfectly at the same time exactly a semitone sharp. He smiled. 'I used to do that' he said, which staggered me as I'd always assumed I was unique. We got back on the stand, and after a couple of numbers he turned to me and said 'watch this' and he did it, there on the stage with the band. Brilliant, but that's only half the point of the story. The other half is that no one in the pub noticed. Now, if they didn't notice a man singing a whole song a semitone sharp, what chance of them noticing the subtle nuances in our playing? And thus I learned an extremely important lesson.

It was during my time with the Firm that I started questioning the way I'd been going about recording for the last few years. I'd had some problems with 'vocal booths' being so padded and soundproofed that they took away what power I had in my voice, so with the Firm I started overdubbing vocals in a passage or in the khazi and it worked out great. Since then I've always looked for the best place to record vocals or certain instruments, and if that's in the corridor or the bog rather than the studio so be it.

I also started having serious second thoughts about the use of headphones (aka 'cans' or 'Desperates'). Remember that Lockjaw business? Well, same thing, it suddenly struck me that while cans allow you to hear everything perfectly you don't *feel* anything at all, and the feel is at least as important, isn't it? Don't answer that. So I started doing all my overdubs in the control room, vocals included, so I could get some feel from the monitor speakers. Don't you get 'track leak' I hear you cry? Yes, you do, now shut up or I'll set the 'spade chicks' on you.

NB: The same applies when you're listening to other people's tracks – if you're listening on cans you don't feel anything, and since most people seem to spend most of the time with cans on their ears you've got to ask if they're not missing out on something important too. In fact I have a theory about that, but I'll get around to it later.

Working in the control room has a second 'fringe benefit' when overdubbing guitar solos, as it means you're not left hanging on your own watching faces through a glass screen, playing solos and hearing 'let's try another one' over and over again until you can't tell your arse from your elbow. If you're in the control room at least you can hear the others saying 'well that was a load of crap' and you know where you stand.

NB: 'Experts' will tell you you can't record vocals this way, you need to be in the studio or vocal booth, wearing cans and using a three-grand specialist vocal microphone with 'pop' shield or it will sound terrible. Well, when Grahame Lister came up with a 'rap' version of 'Arthur Daley' (yes I know, but bear with me) I did the lead vocals in the control room with a hand-held Shure SM58 and I defy anyone to spot the deliberate mistake.

NB (again): I once heard of three classical 'experts' being asked to judge four violins in a 'blind' test, a Stradivarius, a

Guarnieri, a 100-year-old French one and one that was only a year old and made in somewhere like Weybridge. Two of the 'experts' got two out of four right, the third got them all wrong. Experts, you've got to laugh, haven't you?

Meanwhile, back on the ranch, for some reason I can't remember, Gas Company was invited to play at Preston Jazz Club. Jazz group we weren't; in fact I'd based our approach on Rory Gallagher's band which I'd seen a couple of times before we left London, but we did a lot of improvisation and the Preston audience seemed to like it. More importantly for me, I suddenly found myself mixing with jazz musicians, something I'd never got the chance to in London, and I grabbed the opportunity with both hands.

Gary Boyle, one of Britain's best jazz-rock guitarists and an old friend from London, helped to introduce me around, some of the best local jazzers like bebop guitarist Bob Gill, saxist Harold Salisbury and pianist Norman Bolton let me do gigs with them, God bless them, and I spent most of my spare coming to terms, finally, with the great American songbook. I've been learning ever since, and I have to say it's not only the most musically rewarding thing I've ever done – it's also the most FUN! Jazz these days has an 'intellectual' tag hanging round its neck but it's nothing of the sort. It's pure freedom, and if that ain't fun I don't know what is.

As I got more proficient at the old jazz lark I got to play alongside a couple of visiting American jazz guitarists, which was an education and a half. I got to do a couple of tunes with John Pisano at the invitation of Adrian Ingram, one of our better exponents, but the biggest thrill was when Gas Company, which spent a year or two as a jazz quartet, was invited by Blackpool Jazz Club to support the legend that is Tal Farlow.

Gas Company then included Mike Walker on guitar (which was nothing to be ashamed of) and when we'd played our set we settled down to listen to the master at work. Just watching and listening to him was a learning experience par excellence, not just the way he played his solos but the way he comped behind the others in his quartet. (Gary Boyle, who was there that night too, said to me in wonder 'look, he's not just improvising with chords, he's improvising the *chords themselves* as he goes'! He was too).

The biggest thrill, though, came at the end of the night when Tal invited Mike and I to play a number with him. Wow! We decided to play 'Have You Met Miss Jones', sharing verses and middle-eights as we went, but it was always Tal who ended up with the middle-eight, arguably the most difficult section of the tune. On about the third pass he grinned and said 'how come I keep getting the middle-eight'? I smiled back. 'Because you're Tal Farlow' I said.

It was around this time that I invited a friend of mine Roger Whitley, Beatles expert par excellence and father of Scott (more of him later) to come and hear the band. 'Oh I don't like jazz' he said, but I persuaded him with some fancy talk and he loved it so much he told Scott he should see it too. 'Oh I don't like jazz' said Scott, who enjoyed it so much he told his mate 'you should come and hear Tone's band' to which his mate replied 'oh I don't like...' well you get the message.

Which begs the question, what exactly does the phrase 'I don't like jazz' mean? And, more to the point, why do English people say it as a matter of course? How has it become as ingrained in our psyche to say 'I don't like jazz' as to say 'I don't want to catch typhoid' or 'I'd rather not be strangled by a cannibal'? By all means don't like it if you don't want to, but in my experience a lot of people find they *do* like it – very much indeed in some cases – once they're exposed to it, even people who started off by saying 'Oh I don't like jazz'. So why say it?

Seems to me it's like people who have never tasted Indian food saying 'I hate that foreign muck' when you offer them a curry. It's just something they always say because the people around them say it, like people who say they don't like blacks or Asians or Jews or gays or Catholics or Italians. Or musicians for that matter. For some reason the entire English race has been programmed to say 'Oh I don't like jazz' whenever the subject is broached, and I have no idea why or who started it.

But... if my vast experience of the music business has taught me anything it's that the people who run the music business don't like music much and absolutely loathe musicians, because musicians have thoughts, ideas and opinions of their own. What 'they' have always craved is a music business with no musicians in it at all, so that whoever *is* in it will do as they're told when they're told, and that's pretty much what they've now got. Now, this may have no bearing on the 'I don't like jazz' phenomenon but it's an odd coincidence that they've both come along at the same time. Isn't it?

You know, it's often been said that the music business chews people up and spits them out and it's often been true. It's like shark-infested quicksand – what don't bite you in the arse drags you under. I've seen it all my life and sort of put up with it, but the one thing I can't forgive it for is what it did to Amy Winehouse. The trouble with people who have little or no talent is that they don't recognise the real thing when they see it and simply paint it with the same garish colours they use to make their mediocrities sellable. Call me Mr Magic if you like, but I saw it coming the first time I ever heard Amy. I just didn't expect them to do it so soon.

To my great personal satisfaction I did end up getting quite good at playing jazz, but there are limits and some limits are almost impossible to understand. For instance, I bought 'The Incredible Jazz Guitar of Wes Montgomery' when I was sixteen and was blown completely away by it. I felt as if I was in the slime and he was on Venus, which was fair enough at the time. Fifty years later I had managed to get out of the slime and pull myself onto the bank but Wes is still on Venus and there is nothing I can do about it. I think it was Joe Satriani who said 'none of us will ever be able to play like Wes but the point is he's got us all trying' and I couldn't bet it putter myself.

If my own personal 1980s were something of a mixed bag, Old England's 1980s seemed to be a bag of shit whichever way you looked at them. It started with the sinking of the Belgrano by a British submarine and the subsequent pathetic 'oh dear, we've lost the log book, sorry' response from the government, and continued with the release from prison of the Guildford Four, the Birmingham Six, Stefan Kiszko, Judith Ward and God knows who else because they'd been stitched… sorry, wrongfully convicted in the first place.

Yvonne Fletcher, the policewoman killed during the Libyan Embassy siege, was reported to have been shot not by the Libyans but by, or with the compliance of, our own secret service, and during the miners' strike the TV news showed some of the footage of a miners v police confrontation backwards so that it looked like the police were retaliating to an attack by the miners rather than the other way round.

I once spoke to a bloke who had been a copper at one of these standoffs and he told me he recognised his brother in the opposite line of police. The only problem, he said, was that his brother wasn't in the police – he was in the army. It was this ruthless destruction of the miners, I reckon, that finally did for any sense of 'we can win this' amongst us rank-and-file English people, 'cause it was made very clear to us that we couldn't. As in feudal times, the high-ups in the castle made decisions and us peasants outside the walls had to take it or suffer the consequences.

Since then we've had inquiries into press corruption and banking corruption, MPs' expenses scandals, mysterious deaths, a couple of dubious Middle Eastern wars and the entire City of London described as a 'massive cesspit'… you used to be called 'paranoid' if you didn't trust anyone, now you should be sectioned if you do.

In Jay & Lynn's magnificent 'Yes Minister' (or 'Yes Prime Minister', I'm not sure which) Jim Hacker was asked by someone if he should believe a certain rumour he'd heard. 'Has it been officially denied yet'? said Hacker. The man said it hadn't. 'Ah' said Hacker, 'never believe anything until it's been officially denied'. Well, that's my official policy now – whatever they say, assume the opposite.

What's all this got to do with my life story, you may ask? Well, call me old fashioned if you like, but 'no man is an island' and I react badly when it seems that everyone in charge of everything is up to no good, especially when they're *my* everyone. I grew up at a time when the 'baddies' were someone else from somewhere else, foreigners basically, while the British Empire was a shining example of saintly benevolence and good practice, and I don't take kindly to suddenly being a 'baddy' even if it is only by association. It may be true but it fucking hurts, know what I mean?

But… there was one bright spot for me during the '80s and it came courtesy of Midge Ure and Bob Geldoff. Like Woodstock, Live Aid was organised quickly, like Woodstock it carried with it the seed of something positive, and like Woodstock it was musicians who staffed it and made it happen.

I watched all of it and I couldn't have been prouder. It was our lot, up there, doing something fab for a great cause, not because it was expected but because it wasn't. And it had a great tag line too – 'give us your foochun monny' – which I vastly prefer to 'every little helps'. (I always hear it as 'every little helps Tesco' myself. I can't think why). Geldoff was so passionate about it I hoped, deep down, it might actually have a galvanising effect.

Then I heard that for every pound Live Aid put into Africa the western banks were taking two pounds out again in interest. One thing you can be sure of about bankers, if someone found a cure for death itself they'd fuck it up somehow.

I only saw Live Aid on TV, but there was one memorable gig I did attend around this time, and that was to hear Stéfane Grappelli at the Municipal Hall in Colne. He was in his eighties then and still playing like he always had, fast and sweet. But he did one thing I'd been warned about previously, and if you want to know about it you'll have to come back, back, back with me to some years earlier…

It was about 1980 when me and Shirle went to see Chet Atkins in concert in London. Chet's playing was magical, as always, and after the gig I was invited backstage to meet him, a real thrill after all those years. The meeting was brief – just long enough for him to tell me what a big influence I'd been on him – then he put on a white glove and shook my hand. I was a little startled by that. Was he worried I'd steal his technique if our hands touched? Or did he have a premonition about Michael Jackson?

Anyway, a few years later I was doing a guitar workshop with John Etheridge and Gary Boyle when John started regaling us with tales about touring with Stéfane Grappelli, one of which involved the aforementioned Chet Atkins. Chet, it seemed, had invited Grappelli to America and Stéfane had gone and recorded an album with Chet in Nashville.

A few months later John was waiting in an airport lounge with Stefan when who should walk by but Chet. He spotted Stefan, went to say hello and the pair of them chatted for a while before Chet left to catch his plane, at which point Stefan turned to John and said 'who he'? 'Who's *he*'? said John, 'that was Chet Atkins, you just made an album with him' but Stefan, he said, was completely nonplussed. 'That's what he's like' said John, 'can't remember anything'.

I didn't know whether to believe it or not at the time, then I went to see Grappelli at the Colne Muni. The gig was great, as you'd expect, and half way through Stefan began to announce 'Nuages'. 'This next tune' he said 'was written by my old partner in the Quintet of the Hot Club of France, someone I played with for many years and who is widely regarded as the greatest guitarist of all time, er... erm... er...' And he couldn't remember his name. No wonder he couldn't remember Chet. Someone in the audience eventually shouted 'Django Reinhardt', Stefan said 'ah yes, Django', got the best laugh of the night and probably his biggest round of applause, and I've never doubted John Etheridge since.

The Mandroid and Other Tales...

It was while I was doing a gig with Gary Boyle that I met a sometime folk singer and musician called Les Pye, who had come across to see us from his usual stamping ground on the Fylde. I had never even been to a folk club much less played one, and for the hell of it I asked if I might join him on a couple of gigs. I loved it, we got on like a house on fire musically and personally, and having played a few clubs together I ventured the opinion that we should inject a touch of humour into our performances, little dreaming what it would end up leading to.

What it led to, and quite quickly, was the most delightful collaboration I'd ever had with anyone – a two-man theatre company combining sketches (some comic, some quite Becketesque) with musical interludes in a manner, I think, that was utterly unique. We called ourselves Cooger & Dark after the villains in Ray Bradbury's 'Something Wicked This Way Comes' and we played wherever we could find a seated audience.

Cooger & Dark took part in three 'Goon Show Preservation Society' celebrations, two in Preston (organised by the ebullient Paul Geraghty who tragically died not long afterwards) and one in Newcastle-upon-Tyne, and all three were joyful, no other word for it. Each one started with personal comic contributions from Goon lovers of all sorts, some present, some not (a young Stephen Fry sent a taped piece for the first Preston show I remember) and the second half consisted of a 'Goon Show' written and performed by society members themselves.

The Newcastle team, having written their show, actually sent it to Spike Milligan for approval and Spike, being Spike, added some bits of his own before sending it back. The show was based on the painting of the Forth Bridge and I remember one line in it that was definitely Spike – Q: 'what colour are you going to paint the bridge'? A: 'We haven't decided yet, we're still choosing the wallpaper'. Spike is a bit of a god to me so I couldn't have been more at home.

Cooger & Dark also played warm-up for Granada TV's 'The Comedians' (the only one who came up to us afterwards, said thanks and wished us luck was the much-maligned Bernard Manning) and of course we did what all comic acts are obliged to do by law - three weeks at the Edinburgh Fringe. In Edinburgh, luckily. To be honest our shows could have been better attended – they could have been *attended* some nights – but doing the show night after night every night pulled it together quite magically.

Les, I must say, was a bit of a revelation. For someone who had never acted before, or even thought about it, he was great at almost every character he played and mastered the bits of jazz I foisted on him brilliantly too. My old mucker Mike McGann came with us as tour manager and his young mucker Grahame Foote came with us… well, he just came with us.

As anyone who's done it will tell you, accommodation is a pig to find in Edinburgh at Fringe time and we all ended up sleeping in one room of some bloke's house on a council estate, just around the corner from a street called Waugh Path which I thought was brilliant and still do. We got along fabulously, or so I thought until one by one the others started coming to me in quite serious states of distress. 'He's driving me nuts!' was the basic unit of discordant currency and I couldn't understand it at first.

Then it dawned on me – none of them had ever been obliged to share every intimate moment with other people before, whereas I had done eight years of it with Willie's band and the Rubettes. Being a wonderful human being I managed to spread peace and love amongst them, and when I thought about it afterwards I realised that I had always had the opposite problem – working with people *without* knowing them that well. I'm sure this poses tremendous problems for bands the first time they go on a serious tour – being comfortable with that level of intimacy takes time.

We only took in one other show in Edinburgh, an afternoon concert by The Fairer Sax, an all-female quartet of soprano, alto, tenor and baritone saxes who were quite brilliant, but we did get around in our tea half-hours and the best of them was spent at the National Gallery of Scotland. I think it's fair to say our gobs had never been so smacked, and it started in the entrance hall when Grahame whispered 'have you seen that couple over there'? He nodded towards them and said 'I've been watching them for a minute and they haven't moved'. No, well, they couldn't move because they were 'The Tourists' by Duane Hanson, made of fibreglass or some such and so real that while your rational brain was saying 'it's an exhibit' your subconscious was screaming 'stop staring at those people'!

Weird and very impressive. And the more we investigated the place the more impressive it got. Mike fell in love with a bronze by Giacometti called 'Woman with her Throat Cut', I was mesmerised by Picasso's 'Musician's Table' and a couple of Jackson Pollocks (and that's not rhyming slang) and there was a little sketch called 'Sick Child' that was so atmospheric you wanted to run and get help. Stunning, and if you're ever in Edinburgh…

Naturally we spent a lot of time just hanging around, but being creative types we ended up writing or playing word games and some of the offerings had me crying with laughter. For example, when I spotted a road sign reading 'Airport 12' and said 'these sequels are getting ridiculous' it started an avalanche of 'film sequel' ideas that went on for an hour, with 'The Omen' proving such a great film to sequelise (if that's a word) that I can still remember the best answers. They are, in ascending order, the cowboy version (Omen the Range), the English version (Omen Colonial – it used to be a chain store), the Australian version (Omen Away) and my favourite, the third in the German trilogy (Omen Dri). Me, Les and Mike also invented a new word with the aim of trying to get it into common English usage. The word was 'plelk' and no, we didn't.

Cooger & Dark were also two of the contributors to the first-ever Comic Relief 'Red Nose Day' on Radio Lancashire, doing sketches and mock news stories. We got an unexpected bollocking after the show by the station manager for the punch-line to a Spoonerism sketch in which the Rev Spooner is sold the deeds to a landmine in the Rheingold by a trinfidence cockster in the Piss & Wiggle pub (getting the drift? Good).

Spooner is later advised by a police officer that the worths are deedless, and as the officer is leaving he turns to Spooner and asks 'what do you want me to do with the deeds'? To which Spooner replies 'oh…feed the ducks'! We explained that we hadn't actually used any offending words but the manager insisted that 'people would get the meaning'. Of course they would, that was the point. But did he honestly think the people of Lancashire couldn't take it?

While I'm on the point, the next time you hear someone complain about 'bad language' ask them what's 'bad' about it and watch them grope for an answer. Because – fanfare of Goon Show-style trumpets – there isn't one. There never was. When I was a kid I remember asking my dad why people could say 'testicles' on TV but not 'bollocks' and he had no answer either. He tried telling me that some people found it offensive, but when I asked him why he had to admit he had no idea.

That's because *there is no reason*. That's right, folks, 'bad' words are only 'bad' because someone somewhere at some time decreed it so and everyone else fell in behind them for no good reason whatsoever, yet we still outlaw and ban them. One of the worst things about EastEnders is that real cockneys don't tell people to 'push off', and I ache when someone uses a word like 'crap' on daytime TV and the presenters get all flustered and apologetic. Grow up, for fuck sake.

As I observed at the beginning of this tome, Anglo Saxon words are part of my cultural heritage and are often used by my fellow Londoners in perfectly innocent ways. The ultimate taboo word, for instance, is used simply as a synonym for 'bloke' and often as a term of endearment, as in 'ah, look at that poor old cunt, bung him a fiver eh'. And so-called 'swear' words can usefully alter their meaning by the way they're used, too – 'bollocks' can mean 'I disagree' or 'that's rubbish' or 'I'm depressed' or, for that matter, bollocks. Tony Crombie once looked inside a club we were about to work, came back out to the car, said 'shittington fuck bollocks' and I knew exactly what he meant.

Yet the film critic Barry Norman said that he gets more letters of complaint about 'bad language' in movies than about sex and violence combined, which can only mean that some people think it's more acceptable to mow people down with a machine gun than to tell them to fuck off. Now, if people are taking the time and trouble to write letters of complaint about something there is no reason to complain about, what does it say about them? And why do they have the fucking vote?

NB: I say this apropos of nothing, but point of order, brother, the upper classes eff and blind as much and as often as the working classes, and often much better. The only people who don't are the middle classes, which is bizarre considering they aspire to be a class above themselves. So put that in your smoke and pipe it.

As you may have gathered by now, I love comedy. And of course I loved getting laughs (in the right places, obviously) with Cooger & Dark. My all-time favourite line was in a Sherlock Holmes sketch, where Holmes (Les) and Watson are discussing a recent client. It went like this:

HOLMES

Do you remember the woman who came to see us last week, Watson?

WATSON

The nun? Sister Josephine?

HOLMES

Nun, Watson? Then what about these? (*So saying he holds aloft an extremely sexy bra and knickers*).

WATSON

(*Shocked*) – Holmes?! (*Pregnant pause*) - You haven't started *that* again, have you?

Always got a laugh, that one. But the thing that surprised me most about working with Cooger & Dark was that it wasn't the out-and-out comedy stuff I most enjoyed doing. It was the more meaty, atmospheric pieces I relished because they gave me the chance to get my teeth into a character and really engaged the audience.

My favourite of these was probably a police sketch called 'The Interview' in which a vicious, bullying Glaswegian police inspector (me) does everything he can to successfully 'frame' a clearly innocent and inoffensive schoolteacher (Les) for shooting a policeman during a riot the previous evening. It started with the usual sort of 'you say you were home alone last night but can you prove it' insinuations, and as the circumstantial 'evidence' built up you could feel the tension mounting until the inspector landed the killer blow by planting the murder weapon on the teacher, by which time you could almost hear the audience thinking 'shit, this could happen to me'. Which was the whole point of the sketch.

Anyway, one night we had just come off after a successful show when someone came backstage to tell us there were two police officers in the audience and that they wanted to meet us. I'd never even considered that and I thought 'oh God, this is where we get the lecture, what the hell do we say'? Nervously we went out front and met the two police officers, who smiled warmly, shook us by the hand and told us how much they had loved the stitch-up sketch. I was shocked. I think I said something like 'you weren't supposed to love it...' but frankly I was so appalled I can't remember exactly what I said. At least I think I was appalled, either that or flattered. I still haven't quite made my mind up.

We tried everything we could to get TV people to see Cooger & Dark but our gigs were always 'too far out of town' or 'too late'. So we sent some scripts instead to BBC TV in Manchester, and were delighted to get a call from one of its producers asking us to call in for a chat. This we did, and when we told him of our problem of getting people to come and see us he replied 'ah well, you're working too far out of town and too late at night'. We told him we knew that. 'Tell you what' he said, 'if you can do a show in town and within office hours I will guarantee to be there myself or make sure another producer is'.

So… we managed to book a spot at a club called the Green Room, which was just across the road from the BBC and a few minutes' walk from Granada TV, and it was in the afternoon, well within office hours. We sent invites to the Beeb and Granada and nobody came. Then somebody suggested we film the act and send it to TV companies on the old 'if Mohammed won't go to the mountain' principle, and it so happened that one of our biggest fans ran his own video company. Knockout. We filmed about six sketches, he said he just wanted to film another couple of bits and we never heard from him again. Nor did we ever see the footage he had already shot. We never did find out why.

Cooger & Dark felt like a match made in heaven and while we never did get on TV we did have sketches accepted by both ITV and Channel 4. We were invited to go to London and watch some being filmed for Channel 4's 'Comedy Wavelength', and that's the first time I ever saw Paul Merton. He was the link man for the sketches and I thought he was brilliant. Still do. I couldn't speak to him, though – for the first and only time in my life I had total laryngitis. Not a sound. Trust *me*.

Writing, rehearsing and performing those shows was pure delight, almost a dream, and when we did perform them they were better than well-received, but try as we might we could never get the 'right' people to see it and after the video debacle it simply petered out. I had never been so distraught over the demise of anything. I'd left Willie, Tommy, Bill and the Rubettes with some sadness and regret, but the death of Cooger & Dark broke my heart.

NB: 'The Mandroid' was one of Cooger & Dark's darker sketches, hence the title of this section).

NB (again): I have many reasons to feel aggrieved at the antics of former woman and one-time prime-minister Thatcher. I won't list them all as my hard drive has a limited capacity, so I'll stick to the one that got in the way whenever I was talking to anyone about Cooger & Dark. Namely the way she slipped management-speak into what had been normal conversation and thereby changed the meaning of perfectly good English words. In this case, 'partner'.

PMT (pre Margaret Thatcher) if I'd said 'this is my partner Les' everybody would have known roughly what I meant. Since MT that word has become utterly useless for purpose as it now automatically implies 'lover', and though Les and I were close we weren't that close. Now I realise that words sometimes change their meaning, and that's fine as long as we're left with an alternative.

'Gay', for instance, now means 'not heterosexual' rather than 'cheerful' but that's OK as we've still got 'cheerful' and 'happy' to go at. But there is no other non-sexual word for 'partner'. The nearest is 'colleague' but that doesn't imply 'equal' or, for that matter, two-handed. So now we're left in the daftest of quandaries, where two people working together have to call themselves 'me and the bloke I share the work with equally' while 'partner' has usurped perfectly decent (and more precise) words like lover, husband, wife, feller, woman etc etc.

Can you imagine if they did that in songs? 'Me and My Partner', 'I've Got a Partner', 'The Partner I Love', 'Can't Help Loving That Partner of Mine'… you get the drift. So, here's what I say – English management has always been the worst on earth and it's bad enough when they fuck up and/or scotch everything remotely decent and worthy, the least they can do is piss off with their inane posture-rhetoric and leave the language alone. As for you, if you're using words like 'partner' when you mean something else, *STOP IT*. Or may the ghost of George Orwell creep into your room in the dead of night and do appalling things to your duvet!

Journalism at it's best (sic)...

Stuck for what to do next I managed to get a bit of freelance work writing gig reviews for the Guardian. I can't remember how, but while it didn't earn me much money it did bring me face to face with some terrific musicians I would otherwise probably have missed. The first gig I reviewed was by the Big Town Playboys, a band I'd never heard of and knew nothing about. It turned out that they played 1950s-style rhythm & blues, and when I say played I mean *played*. They swung so hard that when the interval came I could hardly walk to the bar, my ankles were aching that much from foot-tapping, and the review I gave them was an uncompromising encomium.

Turns out they were one of Eric Clapton's favourite bands (he booked them for his 25th anniversary gig, I believe) and Jeff Beck recorded and toured with them, so I'm not on my own in rating them. I also got to see, and interview, one of Chicago's own bluesmen Fenton Robinson, whose playing was a trifle unusual in that he didn't bend notes much and phrased as much like a jazz musician as a blues guitarist. I got the impression he didn't much like the raucous way blues was going – he told me 'blues is a language and a language should be spoken, not shouted' and 'if the band gets too loud I just put down my guitar, tell them I'm outta there and leave the stage'. Wise man.

I enjoyed the first few reviews I did, but then I was sent to see someone I really didn't care for and found myself in a real quandary; I couldn't bring myself to bullshit and pretend it was better than it was, but I couldn't bring myself to criticise it either. So, when I found myself in Manchester one day I called into the Guardian office and had a word with the arts editor. He smiled ruefully. 'People who perform themselves don't want to attack other performers' he said, 'whereas people who don't do it themselves are happy to rip someone to bits if they didn't like the show. It's always the same'. I'd never thought of that before, but it explains almost everything about critics. Doesn't it?

I wrote no more Guardian gig reviews after that, but it led by a somewhat circuitous route to my being offered a full-time job with my local paper, the Burnley Express, by its editor Richard Catlow, who turned out to be the third of those three great bosses I mentioned.

Now I must point out that it was never my intention to be a journalist, but I have always been allergic to bullshit and I thought this might help me get to the bottom of stories. Some people think I'm joking when I say I'm allergic to it but I couldn't be more serious. I don't break out in a rash or anything but I get such a powerful emotional reaction it's as much as I can do to stay upright and keep breathing. Obviously I spend a lot of time gasping and holding on to the furniture, but c'est la vie.

There was another reason for taking the job though. Gas Company was great but it wasn't making any money, my jazz work certainly wasn't making any money, I'd rather have had my nuts chewed off by Simon Cowell than go back to the clubs and sales work was out of the question because I didn't want to go to hell when I died. So when Richard offered me wages I gratefully accepted.

I have a soft spot for towns like Burnley, maybe because they're so different from where I was born and brought up. Where London is, and always was, intensely cosmopolitan, the towns of East Lancashire are insular and parochial. While London is a good two thousand years old and filled with every variety of craft and industry, the East Lancs towns burst into life merely a couple of hundred years ago to furnish two products – textiles and coal.

While London has marched on through the great fire, the plague, the Peasants' Revolt, the Gunpowder Plot and the Swinging Sixties and will continue to march on through God knows what, when the mills and the pits went the northern towns found themselves purposeless, which in a historic sense they are. I find that rather romantic in a sad sort of way. It's like they're pining for a lost love, and the fact that that lost love treated them like shit seems to deter them not at all.

London doesn't understand that, but then London knows nothing of what surrounds those towns, which is some of the most beautiful countryside in England. Places like Pendle Hill, which I can see from my front-room window and always fills me with a sense of awe and wonder. Or Hardcastle Craggs, just over the border in Yorkshire, which is so magical in the spring and summer that if you saw a pixie or two you wouldn't bat an eyelid.

Or Howarth, which is not so far from us, home of the Brontë sisters and pretty well untouched by modernity. No Tesco there to uglify and corrupt, just a few characterful shops, inns and tea rooms and a fucking steep hill, all surrounded by the brooding moors of Jane Height and Wuthering Eyres. Drive the equivalent distance of Burnley to Howarth in London and all you see is buildings and traffic. And there's nothing very magical about that.

As a Burnley Express reporter I got to do all the music, arts and show-biz stuff, naturally, but as a general reporter I had to cover every other kind of story as well – court cases, council meetings (every bit as dull as they sound), fires, riots, wedding anniversaries and just about everything else that affected the Burnley area. I did feel slightly peeved about this, as the guy who did sport only did sport which I felt was a mite unfair.

I hate sport, so I may be slightly prejudiced, and one could have argued that there wasn't enough music, arts and show-biz in Burnley to require a dedicated reporter, but one could equally have argued that Burnley was not the epicentre of international sports either and that sport was given more weight than music, the arts and show-biz combined simply because it was SPORT. I didn't say anything though, as I know a lost cause when I see one.

NB: I got to do one final gig review for the Express – Take That. Honest. They were just on the cusp of becoming famous at the time, and they were doing some promotion at a local high school. It was an odd performance, I thought, just five blokes covered in muscles going potty in unison to a few tracks, but the girls liked it and the Take Thats were pleasant enough, if a trifle distracted, when I interviewed them afterwards. I can't remember what I wrote about them but I doubt whether it affected their career one way or the other. Or mine, for that matter.

Where was I? Oh yes. The 'Burnley area' rule was one that was strictly applied. In fact I was so regularly told by the news editor 'it's not in our area' that when I got a call to say there was someone at the front desk who wanted to talk about the environment I said 'tell them it's not in our area'. I don't know if Richard heard it but he would certainly have seen the funny side because he was by far the best thing about working for the Burnley Express.

He was no modernist, Richard. I thought of him as the nicest 19th century man I knew and his support for local history and heritage schemes was unstinting, but the best thing about him was that he loved his job and tried to make sure that he shared that feeling with everyone else in the building. His motto was 'you have to enjoy what you do' and he backed it up with a genuine cheer and warmth that was irresistible. He also came out with the best ad-lib quote I ever heard, one that summed him up and left my argument in tatters. I was looking worried as usual, Richard spotted it and told me to stop worrying. I said he might as well tell the birds not to fly, and we got into a discussion that I was determined to win.

As it happened I had recently read an article about the 'Doomsday Computer' in America which, based on food/population/pollution statistics, had predicted the end of the world in 1999 (it didn't, you're all right) and I imparted this to Richard adding triumphantly 'then we'll all have something to worry about!' He didn't miss a beat. 'Well, let's face it' he said, 'the end of the world's not the end of the world, is it'. I could have kissed him. He had felled me with a perfect mix of joy, truth and spiritual wisdom and I've never been more delighted to lose an argument.

It was during my time at the Burnley Express that the local council became aware of the south's attitude to the north in general – flat hats, whippets, ferrets, 'we are about to land at Burnley airport, please set your watches back thirty years' you know the drill – and Burnley had done nothing to alleviate the situation by burying itself in its past, lacing all its PR with references to weaving, flying shuttles and 'King Cotton'. So the council decided it was time to come up with a new image, one that would show Burnley as a vibrant town with its face set firmly on the future, an idea I completely concurred with until they unveiled the new slogan. You're not going to believe this: it was 'Cotton on to Burnley' complete with a cotton-reel logo. What's the opposite of 'back to the future'?

Three things happened to Clay while I was at the Express, or rather three places. Being diagnosed autistic meant he could no longer stay at his primary school in Burnley, and because there were no specialist centres locally he ended up travelling by taxi every day to Scotforth House, which was almost fifty miles away in Lancaster. If this wasn't bad enough, some of the cab drivers couldn't speak English (one of them couldn't even read the gauges on the dashboard) and if *that* wasn't bad enough after a couple of years Scotforth House was shut down for cruelty in a court case explosive enough to make the national news. Sounds like I'm making it up, doesn't it? I'm not.

Clay, thank God, was moved again, this time to Peterhouse Autistic School in Southport, which turned out to be a blessing because Peterhouse was a fantastic school and turned Clay around almost immediately. It was a five-day-a-week boarder, which saved him the daily grind of travelling, and though we missed him when he was away his improvement was worth its weight in the obvious.

The bad news was that Peterhouse could only keep him until he was nineteen and we had no idea what might happen next, but thanks to advice from the National Autistic Society what happened next was Raby Hall on the Wirral, run by Wirral Autistic Society. Clay loved it the first time he saw it and he's been there ever since. I hate to gush, but it really is perfect in every way and he's flourished there. In fact so perfect is it that their band, the Beathovens, have shared stages with the like of Bob Geldof and Jools Holland as well as entering – and winning – a Liverpool-based 'battle of the bands' contest. With Clay on drums, of course.

Meanwhile, back at the Burnley Express, the 80th anniversary of the Titanic disaster came along during my tenure, and when the paper found out that a local primary school had done a project on it I was told to call them and get some information. So I phoned the school, had a talk with the teacher and got what details I needed for the article and then, as was often my want, I asked a question of my own that I knew the paper wouldn't use, namely were such young children not upset by talk of such a tragic loss of life. The teacher reassured me. No, she said, they dealt with that very well, but they did get upset when she told them that the first-class passengers had first call on the lifeboats. And that's why I think we should lower the voting age to sixteen. And make it the maximum age.

Of all the people I was sent out to interview my favourite was the cartoonist Bill Tidy, who had come to town for a one-man show. He was a delightful bloke and the interview went as planned, but I had a little off-the-record question for him, too, that the paper wouldn't have approved of – what the fuck was someone as famous as Bill Tidy doing in a place like Burnley? He smiled. 'I like meeting ordinary people' he said, and then he told me this story. Some years ago there were major riots in Toxteth, Liverpool, and fearing there may be worse to come some local people sought an audience with the Prime Minister Her Majesty Thatcher. They were granted one and set off for London by train. Meanwhile two personal private secretaries were dispatched from No 10 in an official car to meet them at Euston.

By the time the train arrived it was late (hard to believe I know) and to make matters worse the official car immediately got stuck in traffic. Panicking, one of the PPSs suggested they take a cab, until one of the Scousers pointed out that the cab would be stuck in the same traffic jam and suggested they all take the tube instead. So out of the car they piled and down into Euston underground station, where they found the platform was jam-packed with people. One of the

Scousers remarked ' the state of this we'll be lucky to get on the train' and one of the PPSs in all seriousness replied (and Bill swore this was true) 'don't worry, when it comes we'll go in the restaurant car'. That, he said was how in-touch 'these people' were, and that was why he liked meeting ordinary folk.

These were examples of the upsides of working for the Burnley Express, but - you knew there was a 'but' coming, right? - the downsides were beginning to get to me. I hated having to publicise the plight of hopeless young scroats up in court for stupid little crimes, or single mothers fined for stealing Pampers from Boots (if they couldn't afford the Pampers how were they supposed to pay the fine?). I hated pushing a notebook under the nose of someone whose home had just burnt down or cross-examining some poor bloke whose wife had just died in childbirth – the whole thing was too intrusive and, if I'm honest, I just wasn't nosy enough and like an idiot I drifted back to the bottle to make it bearable.

It didn't work of course. It just made it worse, and the final showdown came one night when Shirle and I had a flaming row and I walked out. Such was my emotional turmoil I had no idea where I was going apart from a vague and frankly mental notion of walking to the Wirral to be near Clay, though what I expected to do there I had no clue. Be a bum, I guess. In fact I got no further than about ten miles before I turned round and walked back into Burnley centre, turning up at the Burnley Express office just after it opened. I had to quit the job almost immediately on health grounds and ended up on Incapacity Benefit.

NB: The title of this chapter is a headline that actually appeared in the Burnley Express, but not, unfortunately, in an article about how to shoot yourself in the foot.

I was in a right state by then and my own doctor and at least three consultants had all affirmed that I was suffering from severe depression and acute anxiety, but the government wanted to get people off Incapacity Benefit and to this end I was sent to a government doctor who pronounced me fit for work. Of course he did. That's what he was there for. If you'd taken him a three-day-old corpse he would have pronounced it fit for work. God knows what state you'd have had to be in for him to pronounce you unfit for work – in an urn, presumably.

You know, it's truly staggering what a qualified doctor, Hypocratic Oath and all that, will do for money at the behest of a corrupt government. Maybe Harold Shipman wasn't a psychopathic serial killer after all, perhaps he was just being paid by the government to get people off the state pension. At least that would make some sense of it. (My Uncle Ern has a phrase – 'kill the cripples first'. I think it comes from the Second World War but the way they carry on it might just be current government policy).

As a result of the government doctor's report my benefits were stopped and I was forced to sell most of the records I'd spent a lifetime collecting just to buy groceries. Of course I appealed the decision, and at the appeal hearing the government doctor's evidence was so full of holes that my benefits were restored. Justice done, but my precious records were gone and there was no getting them back. Let me make it clear to anyone who hasn't sussed it yet – governments are bastards.

Backtrack a little – towards the end of my Burnley Express days I was taking lunch in the Burnley Mechanics bar and talking to one of the regulars when he spotted a girl at the next table reading a book about psychology. He asked me if I knew what it was. Oh yes, I told him, I knew what it was and it didn't work.

Clearly unsatisfied with this answer he turned to the girl and asked her. Long story short, she ended up sitting at our table, and when I recounted my own experiences of NHS psychotherapy (have you ever noticed that 'psychotherapist' can also be pronounced 'psycho the rapist'? Just thought I'd mention it) she said 'you should talk to my father' and gave me his number. Forward track a bit, and following my departure from the Burnley Express, and sick and tired of being sick and tired (and out of other options) I called the girl's father, and what happened next was little short of magic.

Darrel Strawson-Sykes was a complex man to describe in a few words. A Buddhist by religion, he was widely-travelled, well-read (particularly about psychology and philosophy) and had spent many years in India where he had learned much about the human psyche and spirit. I warned him about doing the working men's clubs too but I think he'd worked that one out for himself. The first time we met he asked me what I was prepared to do to be cured, I told him 'anything' and he said 'OK, I'll help you'. Then I told him about my decades under the NHS and he wiped it away with a phrase: 'They don't practise causation therapy' he said, 'of course they couldn't cure you'. You know, sometimes you hear a phrase that makes so much sense you wonder why you never heard it before.

And so we started, meeting roughly once a week. Darrell took me through all my past experiences and made me relive them and, eventually, come to completely new terms with them. He asked me what was giving the 'black beast' inside me its power and made me see that I was. He told me I could be an entirely different person in a heartbeat if I decided to. I told him it wasn't that simple. Yes, he said, it is. He asked me if I wanted to come back in another lifetime and live all my bad experiences over again, and when I told him I didn't he said 'then get it right this time'. When I said I felt some particular way or intended to do some particular thing, Darrell never asked 'why'? He always said 'to what purpose'? Which demanded an answer and made me think more than 'why' had ever done.

I once told Darrell about my mirror problem and the 'alter ego' I expected to see looking back at me. It had clarified a bit in my mind by then – a thin, almost gaunt face draped by long, straight blonde hair – and he didn't miss a beat. 'I'm not prepared to talk about past lives yet' he said, as if he knew exactly what I was talking about. Now my reincarnation jury is still out, but I'd give anything to ask him if he was prepared to talk about it now. Unfortunately I can't.

Darrell was deep and deeply spiritual and possessed of tremendous wisdom. I can get pretty far-out myself sometimes, but I never made a point or asked a question that he hadn't examined and considered before. Nothing fazed him. And within a couple of months he had done what no one else had been able to do in the previous forty years. He took my depression away. And he didn't charge me a penny for it.

Strangely, when I thought about it afterwards I realised that one of the most important things he ever did for me was tell me I was right. Not about everything, obviously, but sometimes I'd say something to him and he'd say 'yes, you're right'. The first time it happened it actually knocked me back in my seat and it dawned on me afterwards that no one had ever said that to me before. I don't know what it says about our culture, but it reminds me of something Quentin Crisp said that answered a question I'd been pondering fruitlessly for years. Bear with me. I had spent my life standing on bandstands and stages observing people at their leisure, and I had come to the conclusion that there is no more ridiculous sight on earth than the sight of English people *trying* to enjoy themselves.

They put a lot of effort into it, but they don't seem to be able to manage it until they've drunk enough, by which time they're just pissed. 'Why?' was the question I'd been pondering, and then I heard Crisp. He spent the last twenty years of his life living in New York and he said that while

English people had no problem with the American constitution's 'right to life and liberty' they didn't seem to understand the 'pursuit of happiness' bit. He went on, and I quote as closely as I can, 'having lived in London for thirty years I know why. The English don't want to be happy – they want to be *right*'. Question answered.

Early on in my sessions with Darrell he asked if I'd read 'Illusions' by Richard Bach. I said I hadn't. 'Do!' he said. So I did, and for months afterwards it seemed like every book I needed to complete my spiritual renewal simply fell in my lap - 'Dangerous Prayer' by Rev J. O'Malley, 'An Evil Cradling' by Brian Keenan, 'Mere Christianity' by C.S. Lewis and plenty more just turned up where I happened to be as if I was being handed them, which of course I'm sure I was.

Thanks to Darrell I also discovered a diet that actually worked. I wasn't looking for one, but Dazza happened to notice my considerable capacity for burping and farting and suggested I might be intolerant to some foods. 'Cut out food completely for a few days' he said, 'just drink water. Then start eating again but just rice at first, introduce different foods one at a time and you'll find out which ones disagree with you'. It was perfect advice and of course I didn't take it.

But I did cut out a lot of things I was suspicious of. I cut out meat, bread, sugar, cheese and milk, and instead ate lots of tuna, vegetables and bananas. I still ate fish and chips and the occasional packet of crisps, and I'd have all the Sunday roast except the meat. Well, the weight dropped off me. It was miraculous, so miraculous that when I visited my doctor for the first time in ages he stared at me in shock. 'Did you lose all the weight deliberately'? he said and I told him what I'd been eating. 'Oh good' he said – I'm certain he thought I was dying.

Now I've heard about diets, of course I have, but I've never come across one that's so simple to do. I got used to it almost overnight, and it seemed I could eat as much as I wanted because I never went hungry, yet the weight just fell away. Yes of *course* I should have published it. I should also have stuck to it. The only reason I didn't was that Shirle was a phenomenal cook (still is) and I think she got pissed off cooking stuff I wasn't eating.

I also got involved around this time with East Lancs into Employment, a local project aimed at getting fucked-up people like me back into work. But ELE wasn't your usual brow-beating 'stop skiving' sort of place, it was warm and welcoming and its staff went out of their way to be helpful and supportive – you know, the kind of place you knew the government would shut down as soon as they possibly could.

It was also during this period (keep up) that I started hosting Sunday night 'jam sessions' at the recently-opened Rhythm Station club in nearby Rawtenstall (pronounced Rottenstall) which was part-owned by former Moody Blues and Wings guitarist Denny Laine. And if you think all this sounds confusing believe me it was a damned sight more confusing for me.

The Rhythm Station had been built brand new and for the best possible motives – to attract and present 'name' performers, an aim it singularly failed to achieve. Still it was nice and well-equipped and the Sunday nights thrived, with the odd 'name' musician like Jerry Donahue, my old guvnor Wee Willie and, in the early days, Denny himself, dropping by for a tune or two.

At the same time (keep up) Gas Company (remember them?) had recruited a new member in guitarist Brian Catterall, a real blues authority and an extremely authoritative blues musician who played economically and with real feel, and ELE allowed the two of us to stage a blues evening at their premises which went extremely well. I could have learned a lot from Brian about playing the blues but my latent tendency to overplay everything got in the way. Still, I'm a better player because of him.

Incidentally, most musicians have a second little talent hiding away somewhere. I, for instance, can write a bit, and if you're shaking your head right about now I can only apologise. Brian's other gift was art, and it wasn't little. One Christmas I got a tubular package in the post and I opened it to find a portrait of Jesus Christ, done in chalk on dark blue paper. There can't have been more than a few dozen chalk marks in total, and the effect was (is) astonishing. It still has pride of place above my mantelpiece and it ain't going nowhere.

Meanwhile, back at the Rhythm Station, I found myself sharing a Sunday-night stage with another fine guitarist, Ken

Bradshaw, who was one of the most lyrical players I'd ever heard. Along with my own jazz studies, these two guitarists played a big part in my musical development at that point and I am forever grateful.

I was also grateful to Denny Laine who, having heard me play at the club, told me he had his own studio in Whalley and that I was welcome to use it, free, whenever he wasn't using it himself, a magnanimous gesture I took immediate advantage of by laying down tracks for an album. What album I had no idea, but one doesn't look a gift-horse etc. It didn't take me long to accumulate the requisite number of tracks, I called the album 'Illusions and Dangerous Prayer', the chaps and chapesses at ELE helped out enormously by doing the artwork for it and… voila! Another album that was never released.

Denny also invited me to play with him at a festival in Tonbridge Wells in Kent, which I have to say was a joy on both counts – Denny was the ultimate professional and a lovely bloke. The rehearsals were a walk in the park because he had a wealth of experience and knew his stuff, it was a pleasure for me to spend time with someone who had been around as long as I had, and it was a bit of a thrill to be playing Wings tracks like 'Jet' and 'Mull of Kintyre' with someone who had actually been in Wings.

You know the first time I heard 'Mull of Kintyre' on the radio I was convinced they were singing 'Bollocking Tired'. That's interesting, I thought. And it would have been too. Unfortunately for me (but no doubt fortunately for him)

Denny took off to the States not long afterwards and was never seen again.

Incidentally, one of the guest musicians to grace the stage of the Rhythm Station was our Clay, and as usual I just let him set up a groove and we ad-libbed around him. But one night the regular drummer, who also managed the club, failed to return to the stage, leaving Clay to play for the other guest performers too. He didn't miss a trick for forty-five minutes, so much so that our bass player, Bert Edwards, told me 'I was watching him all the time – he was ear'oling everything, amazing!' Yes, well, that's my boy. The only downside was that Clay had never played drums for forty-five minutes at a stretch and he ended up with leg-ache and blisters.

Backtrack (sorry about this) – from the moment Cooger & Dark took its 'theatre company' shape our manager had been Mike McGann. Mike was president of Preston Jazz Club during the early Gas Company period and we had been friends ever since, but Mike was also a member of Dark Horse Theatre Company and hence... well, theatrical. Since then he had formed his own group, Suspect Theatre, to perform murder nights and he called one day to ask me if I'd be interested in doing one of them. Knowing Mike, and knowing his writing was terrific (very well-read, erudite man, Mike) I jumped at it and on the evening of the inaugural National Lottery I inaugurated myself with Suspect Theatre.

Now I don't know if you've ever done one, but they really are a joy to do. You act out a couple of scenes, in character, get cross-examined by the audience – in character – play

230

another couple of scenes, get cross-examined again, and after the final reveal you go out and meet the audience, by which time you feel like you know everybody. It's *ace,* and if you're not doing it, *why* not? It was probably Mike, too, who first got me thinking seriously about Shakespeare. I'd done Shakespeare at school, of course, but that only made me think seriously about how I could get away with murdering the bloke who was teaching us the Shakespeare.

A Little Learning...

ELE, meanwhile, were trying to find me something constructive (and permanent) to do, and to this end their proprietor, the fab Jean Weaver, pointed out an ad in the paper saying 'musicians wanted for teacher training course'. I wasn't impressed. I had been on so-called 'training courses' before and found them to be a complete waste of everybody's time, but at Jean's persuading I called the number, an audition was arranged and a few days later I found myself sitting, guitar in hand, in front of Access to Music's John Ridgeon and his right-hand woman Hazel. I played a couple of things, had a quick chat about experience and all, and John said he was happy to accept me on the course. Whether I would be happy was yet to be seen, but first I had to get to the course venue in Preston and that depended on the car that dependability forgot, our Mini.

We'd been quite pleased when we bought it. We had a Metro before that but someone rear-ended it at 30mph with us in it and wrote it off. It didn't say in the log book that the Mini had previously been part of the show in Billy Smart's Circus but it might as well have done. If it started at all the window fell off or the wipers wouldn't work, if the brakes worked at all they pulled to one side, if it rained the engine cut out (which was a right laugh in the middle lane of a crowded motorway doing 70) and Shirle and I enjoyed some lovely winter journeys to visit Clay at Scotforth House and Peterhouse because the heater never worked at all.

Of course the bloody thing did let me down a couple of times during the ATM course, but the course itself was heaven. We had fantastic workshops on vocals, percussion and improvisation, all delivered by people who clearly knew what they were doing, and we were treated with the utmost consideration and respect because we were musicians. Not 'in spite of' you'll notice, but because. This had never happened to me before and soon wouldn't happen again, but it was an oasis for a while and God bless ATM for that.

There were a lot of good players on the course, but the star for me was a bloke called Jeff Roberts, who called himself a 'blues archaeologist' but was far, far more than that. Armed with an acoustic or a National Resophonic guitar he could play – and sing – Delta blues like a native, not just slavish copies like some of our 'name' players but with his own original touches and approach.

Anyone who has tried to play plausible Delta blues, especially of the Robert Johnson ilk, will know it's the wrong end of impossible, but Jeff (aka Barbecue Bob Roberts) could even do a convincing version of 'Hellhound on My Trail', a tune I've never gotten close to. Jeff guested with Gas Company a few times and Brian Catterall described his performances as 'like being there'. If Jeff had been American he'd be rich, I reckon. But he wasn't so he isn't.

Anyway, a couple of months into the course I was asked if I would be interested in teaching for ATM. I had seldom felt so flattered and agreed without hesitation. I had tremendous respect for John Ridgeon and everything he stood for so why

233

not? First, though, I had to finish the course with some school-based training and that proved an eye-opener in a couple of different ways.

I started off in a school in Burnley, handy geographically but more than a mite challenging. The kids I was assigned were ten or eleven year old Asians, all Tupac Shakur fans, none of whom had ever had a music lesson in their lives, and my first task was to come up with something basic to get them involved. So I recorded little snippets of John Lee Hooker, Miles Davis, Mozart and Elvis, played them to the kids and asked them to write down what kinds of music they were. They listened attentively to Hooker, Miles and Mozart, but as soon as 'Jailhouse Rock' kicked in they all leapt to their feet and started boogying. I couldn't believe it - thirty little Asian Tupac Shakur fans were going nuts to a fifty-year-old rock 'n' roll track, and if that don't prove something I don't know what does.

I also tried taking a live band into that school, and when our opening tune got very muted applause I assumed it just wasn't their thing. The second tune, though, went better, and after our third offering we got cheers, claps, the full monty. It was a strange reaction until someone pointed out that these kids had never seen anyone play an instrument 'live' before and had been too shocked at first to clap, cheer or do anything much else.

Now, you don't think about things like this until you're obliged to, but I realised then that kids under eighteen don't get much chance to see 'live' music these days because every venue has a drinks licence, while back in the days of the 2Is, the Marquee and the Cavern kids as young as twelve or fourteen could watch live bands pretty much whenever they liked. Think about it.

These experiences were interesting but they were far too limited to be much use to my training, so after a few weeks ATM transferred me to Calder Vale High School in Mytholmroyd (don't ask me how to pronounce it) in Yorkshire. (The town was as small as it sounds, though interestingly I believe it had once been home to Patrick Stewart, who of course moved on from there to Hollywood and then to outer space. 'To Mytholmroyd and beyond' as they say).

At Calder Vale I found myself in the care of music teacher Giselle Finney, and if there's such a thing as a genius teacher Giselle was it. When I arrived she was taking a large class of students through 'The Rhythm of Life' from the musical 'Sweet Charity', splitting them into three groups and trying to play the piano, get them singing and demonstrating the choreography all at the same time. I immediately offered some guitar backing for her, which left her free to sing, dance, encourage and direct, all of which she did with the kind of aplomb deserving of a TV series. She was brilliant at what she did, brilliant with the kids, and you could tell straight away that the kids loved her. I could only watch and feel very inadequate indeed.

Giselle also ran the school choir, and not like anyone else would run it. She knew her harmony, knew how to inspire and arrange, and she went out of her way to find fresh, interesting things for the kids to sing. One of these had a little touch of genius of its own. I don't remember who wrote it, but it was quite modern harmonically and the lyrics, get this, were in mock Latin – just nonsense syllables that sounded gorgeous and, somehow, significant. As always, I could only look on in awe at Giselle in full flow. To me she was inspirational and intimidating all in one go and it was a privilege to witness it. I believe she eventually left Calder View to join ATM, which must have been a shocking blow to those students. I mean, shocking.

School-based training done and dusted it was time to start my own teaching career, and the first priority was to get shot of Coco the Clown's car. I would only be doing a couple of days a week to start with, but ATM was expanding and Shirle and I reckoned we could manage £30 a week so we part-exed the nightmare for a second-hand Nissan Micra. It was red, Shirle nicknamed it Gabby (short for the Angel Gabriel as it felt like a Godsend) – its licence plate even started with 'L5' – it was paradise. It started, went, didn't stop when it felt like it and things weren't constantly breaking down or falling off (come on, you don't get stuff like this on 'Top Gear').

And so my teaching career started. For the first year or two I did sessions at Blackburn, Dewsbury, Warrington and Manchester and the odd one-day workshop on other ATM training courses until Blackburn got enough students under its belt to retain my services exclusively. I was never coining it in (the hours varied every year but I never earned more than about half the average wage) but I was working, and doing it for someone who believed in me. For a while it felt like being reborn.

Now let me make one thing clear at this point – I have never believed that you can 'teach' music. Reading you can teach, or writing, or adding up, or driving, or languages because they are skills and therefore acquirable by most people. But music is an art and that's not. Call it a gift, a talent or a vocation, it's either innate or it ain't, you either got it or you don't. My mate Mike McGann is the most intelligent, intellectual person I know and he *loves* his music but all his attempts at mastering an instrument have fallen on stony ground. Stephen Fry likewise - they don't come much brighter than him, but he can't play two notes worth hearing and it drives him *crazy*. He don't got it either. Only people that have got it get it, got it? Good. So why 'teach' it then?

Well, while you can't teach it you can *coach* it and that was John Ridgeon's basic concept for ATM. It should be free of any constraints, on students or tutors, thus allowing open learning that suited the learner. No exams – students were marked on a performance at the end of each year and that performance could be pretty well tailored to suit the student. So the first couple of years were a learning curve for all of us, with students learning to play and tutors learning to teach at the same time, an excellent state of affairs.

But – you knew there would be a 'but' coming, right? – deep down in the English psyche there's a little voice that keeps whispering things like 'don't leave well enough alone 'and 'if it ain't broke, break it' (I'm so convinced this should be the English national motto that I've translated it into Latin for you – it's '*si non fregit frangeret*'. Now all we need is a consensus. Who's with me?) and sure enough the day came when the education authorities (whoever they are) asked ATM where its criteria was, ATM said 'we don't have any' and the education authorities replied 'no criteria, no funding'. This led ATM to come up with some criteria fast, and as we all know when you throw something together quickly you come up with… well, you know. Once it's done, though, you're stuck with it and everybody is obliged to use it. Mistake No. 1.

Mistake No. 2 came when the government, in its infinite (no, wait a minute, not infinite, erm… non-existant, that's it) wisdom decreed that ATM could no longer franchise its courses to colleges. I don't begin to understand the full implications of this, all I know is that suddenly I was no longer employed by the people who had employed me – you know, the people I trusted and respected and who trusted and respected me – but was now in the employ of Blackburn College instead. Oh well, all you can do is get on with it and for a while it was at least sort-of get on withable. (Or is it 'get onable with'? Sometimes the finer points of the English language elude me).

The ability of the students I found myself teaching varied enormously, as you'd expect; they had different talents (or lack of them), different agendas and they learned in different ways and at different rates. But they almost all had two things in common – a 'just left secondary school' repression and an almost total disinterest in what was in the charts. Both of these were understandable up to a point – I've long believed that the English education system is aimed at the old military idea of 'break their spirits and they'll obey without question' and why would you be interested in what was in the charts when what was in the charts was so… well, naff? Bill Bailey said there's more evil in the charts than in an Al-Qaeda suggestion box and he's right.

But… those two things are both wrong on a fundamental level. If young musicians aren't interested in what's in the charts, WHO IS? Who's buying this stuff? When I was a young musician we were *nailed* to the charts, from Elvis through the Beatles to Cream and Hendrix, and here was a chart system with no appeal to young musicians. This, you may say, is neither here nor there, but it meant there was no common frame of reference among most of my students. We couldn't jam over the same piece of music because everyone was listening to something different, and the ability to jam is crucial.

As for the education system, deliberately robbing young people of their sense of self-worth should be against the Geneva Convention, and it is deliberate. I'll tell you how I know. The Rubettes once took part in a live Jimmy Saville radio talk show for which the entire studio audience were Eton students, all in uniform, from the littlest ones right up to the biggest ones, and I was staggered, staggered I was, at their self-assurance.

Invited to give their opinions, kids of, I don't know, ten or eleven stood up (or as up as they could get) and spoke with the maturity, eloquence and self-confidence of an ambassador or captain of industry and I thought 'hang about a minute, *these* kids haven't been repressed'. I might not have agreed with everything they said, but they had been raised to say it with absolute self-assurance and suddenly the state education the rest of us were obliged to endure looked very tacky and dubious indeed. Is it really deliberately aimed at keeping us 'in our place'? There's no doubt in my mind.

I might be stating the bleeding obvious here, but while you could be forgiven for assuming that colleges and universities are manned by the brightest people available the reverse is often the case. For example, I was once walking into Blackburn College with one of our former students, Jon Bond, when a tutor from another department spotted him and said 'wow, you look completely different'. Now, if he looked completely different, *how did he know it was him*? Eh?

More to the point, when I took the mandatory CertEd course it was explained to us that the government's main objective was to 'attract back to education those who had been put off it in the past', i.e. working class people from poor backgrounds. I said that, in order to comply with this particular objective, the college should replace its flash reception counters with sofas, and rather than ask prospective students to fill in forms they should invite them to make themselves comfortable and ask them if they fancied a cup of tea, but I added that I thought it unlikely as the college would never abandon its 'we're cleverer than you' image. This, I was told, was quite accurate. See? Thick.

The next thing I noticed, however, wasn't about the college or my students. It was about me. I was playing the love theme from the 'Godfather' one day when I noticed something strange: it was totally lacking in expression. Dull, flat and lifeless it was, and I couldn't understand why. I was *trying* to express it but nothing I tried made any difference. Now, Darrell had always told me two things – never *try* to do anything, either do it or don't do it but never *try*. And if you need the answer to a serious question don't *think* about it, ask for the answer and keep asking. Ask who, you may say? Well, being a Buddhist Darrell was loath to use the word 'God': he would just imply something like a great spiritual consciousness, but either way you put the question out there and wait for an answer. It could be a long time coming, just keep asking.

Now this probably seems 'new-agey' and a bit cosmic, but Darrell never told me anything wrong, so I did what he suggested. Night and day I kept asking 'why' and the answer hit me like a ton of bricks six months later while I was painting the bathroom wall at home. And here's the answer. My adolescence, as you've heard, was little short of nightmarish; its only saving grace was my guitar playing, and one day my playing had impressed someone and a switch had been thrown in my head that said 'if you want a positive reaction, impress people'. Since that day, without realising it, that's what I'd been trying to do every time I played. Not touch people or move people, but impress them.

This sudden realisation (what Darrell would call a 'cognisence') left me reeling, so much so that for days I dare not touch the guitar. When I did – and I had to, I had a gig – I felt myself doing things I had been doing for decades without realising it; playing something and looking round to see if anyone was impressed. And guess what? The problem evaporated, went away. A bit late in the day, I thought, but it had gone and it never came back. Darrell-power! It shows, though, how many things we do through some sort of 'programming' that we're quite unconscious of, and if we ain't got a Darrell to unlock them for us we can quite easily go to the grave without ever realising it.

NB: Apropos of that, I came across a little brain-teaser around this time that scared the shit out of me, and I'm happy to share it with you. It runs thus; there's a black dog on a black tarmac road and there's a car coming. There are no street lights, none of the houses along the road has any lights on and neither does the car, how does it avoid hitting the dog? I've never known anyone get the answer right without help: the answer is that it's broad daylight. Now no one has told us it's night time but we assume it because of the 'no lights' bits, which begs the question – how many times during the rest of an average day do we 'assume' things that may be wrong and make decisions based on it? Scary, eh?

Speaking of which, Shirle had got herself a job as a nursing assistant while I was at college. I had a day off, and as she was due home after a morning shift I put the TV on for her. It looked for a moment as if a plane had hit one of the towers of the World Trade Centre in New York, and I was just in time to see a second plane hit the other one. Some events just stop time for you, even if you're not involved in them yourself, and time stopped for me.

When Shirle got in a few minutes later she said she'd heard something about it on the radio in the car but it didn't make much sense. No, well... for the rest of the day we did nothing but watch events unfolding, live, and when the towers fell part of me disintegrated with them.

I felt such enormous empathy with the confused and terrified New Yorkers, obviously, but on top of that was an overwhelming feeling of awe. Awe at the sheer genius of it – did they know the attack would bring the towers down, and if so *how*? Awe at the audacity of picking that particular target, which must have looked to them like the wealthiest in the west sticking two fingers up at them. And awe at the pure evil of ploughing planes full of innocent passengers into buildings full of innocent workers.

Of course the conspiracy theories have raged ever since, with or without foundation I've no idea, though the fact that I wouldn't put it past them bothers me deeply. But there was a question I heard a number of New Yorkers ask while it was all happening, a question I thought was a fine one, namely 'what have we done to make them hate us so much'? Yes, I thought, keep asking that one and maybe some good might come out of this, but I've never heard anyone ask it since. Not once.

9/11 left me in a state of shock, my head reeling with questions, my heart breaking in sympathy with everybody involved, from the passengers on the planes to the people in

243

the towers, the emergency services and the people of New York themselves, who had not experienced anything like it on home soil since the Civil War. If I ever got over it it certainly took months, but I'm not sure I ever did. Perhaps if they'd just kept asking that fucking question…

Back at college I met and coached some terrific young chaps, some of whom are still friends years later. Unfortunately the college couldn't do enough for us so they didn't bother, and year on year the amount of prescriptive criteria increased exponentially (most of it a waste of everybody's time) so that I found myself trying (that word again) to teach the guitar in spite of the criteria rather than because of it.

But I became increasingly aware that neither of these things was working. The criteria – scales, modes and the like – achieved nothing because that's not how a musician plays, and you don't retain them anyway without a frame of reference to put them in.

But my own personal tuition wasn't having an effect either for the same reason - you needed a framework of tunes to make sense of them and my students knew no tunes. What they knew were simple chords, riffs, so-called 'power' chords and minor pentatonic scales – the stuff of rock music, in other words, and I realised as the time went by that you learn nothing worth knowing from rock music.

WHAT? I hear your strangled cry, but rock music ROCKS, man, what are you talking about? Well… did you ever see the edition of 'QI' that dealt with rabbit meat? It seems that old American hunters and trappers were dropping like flies from malnutrition in spite of filling their bellies every day with rabbit, and nobody could understand it.

It turned out that rabbit tasted fine but there was absolutely no nutrition in it – at all – so if all you ate was rabbit you effectively died of starvation. That's rock music in a nut case. Truth is there's more nutrition in one chorus of 'I Do Like to be Beside the Seaside' than there is in half a dozen rock albums or three years of 'criteria' but colleges and universities persist in teaching the criteria/theoretical route because it suits them. This used to be bad enough when it was free. Now they're charging for it it's little short of fraud. Sorry.

They do this in the name of 'qualifications' but let's get one thing straight right now – in the world of contemporary music, qualifications are meaningless. If someone wants a guitar player and you turn up for the audition, all they want to know is whether you can do it or not. If you can you get the gig, if you can't you don't. You can have a truck parked outside loaded down with your qualifications and no one will give a toss. Colleges and universities say they 'care about their students' but if they really cared about them they would show them how to acquire the tools to make themselves as effective as possible in the real world.

Like Albert Lee, for instance. He'd worked all over England in virtual obscurity for twenty years and only went to Nashville for a two week holiday because he thought he owed it to himself to see the real thing. Within two days of his arrival he was making an album with the Crickets, and when James Burton left Emmylou Harris's Hot Band Albert got the gig. How? By being able to jam instantly with any band, by ear, and make it sound as if he'd been with them for months. That's how musicians open doors, and that's what colleges and universities should be helping young musicians to do. No doubt qualifications please Ofsted and boost the college's league-table ratings but they are worthless to the students. Does that sound ethical to you?

So, you ask, did we produce no good players at Blackburn College? It depends how you look at it. Some fine players came out of it, but it had little or nothing to do with the course. Take Roo Walker, for instance, a terrific talent with improvisational skills to marvel at and great feel to boot, but Roo was immensely gifted before he started on the course and that's no credit to us. (I advised Roo to specialise in jazz, on the grounds that while there wasn't much money in it there weren't many young guitarists either and he'd have the field almost to himself, but he told me jazz was 'too hard'. Pillock).

Or take Jordan Westwell, for instance, who did well but not spectacularly on the course and then came back six months later a different player – he'd done the work on his own and done it brilliantly. He could play 'Apache' light years better than I could and I'd been doing it three times longer than he'd been alive!

Or take bassist Greg Harper, a fifty- year-old man in an eighteen-year-old body whose insides refused to let him do anything wrong, a very rare gift indeed. Or Tom Carr, a piano student who only needed the basics of jazz opened up for him to take off like a rocket on his own. I could go on but you get the drift. I never thought of myself as a great teacher but I introduced students to the music of some great musicians they'd never listened to before, and I had enough experience to answer almost any question and illuminate my answers with personal examples.

One strange anomaly I spotted at college was the lack of female students. We had some, naturally, but almost all of them sang. Virtually none of them played an instrument. We would often start off with a handful of guitarists or bassists, but within weeks most of them had given up. In fact in thirteen years I only ever had two girls complete the course, and that is pretty well par for the course (no pun intended) in music generally. Or in contemporary music anyway – there always seems to be a fair ratio of women to men in a symphony orchestra. What stops them playing rock or jazz, reggae or country music?

I raise the issue because I have heard women talk of 'sexism' in the music business and that's bollocks. Musicians are, by nature and inclination, the most anti-racist, anti-sexist mob on the face of the planet and always have been.

They were defying racism and segregation long before Martin Luther King and the Civil Rights movement. In the 1920s and 30s, behind closed doors, Bix Beiderbeck and Louis Armstrong jammed together. Eddie Lang and Lonnie Johnson recorded together (though Eddie Lang was listed as Blind Willie Dunn) and Alan Freed was persecuted for putting black and white bands on the same stages in the 1950s.

Likewise, women have always played a major role in music and I never heard any musician, ever, complain about it. Why would they? If the fairer sex have done this almost exclusively as singers that's their prerogative, and I never heard any musician complain about that either. If few women choose to play it ain't because anyone's boycotting them or putting them off. I'd be interested to discover the real reason, but sexism? Do me a favour.

I had been at Blackburn College for a few years when by pure coincidence I was asked to do an interview on Radio Lancashire. I can't remember why, but during the course of the interview the presenter, Tony Livesey, made mention of the number of former 'pop' stars there were in Lancashire and suggested, jokingly I think, that they should get together and make a Christmas record. I thought nothing of it at the time, but when I got home I started writing one and it occurred to me that it could be a great project for the music course. We could involve some tutors and students in the making of it, the rest of the students would see a 'professional' project being done, it could make great PR for the college and might even raise a few bob for the course.

So I roped in composition tutor Iain Reddy to play some guitar (great guitarist, Iain) and bass tutor Scot Whitley to play bass and produce the thing, as well as student Adam Swarbrick to do the lead vocal and a student 'choir' for the chorus. We did basic recording 'in house' at the college, then

Scott and I did the overdubs and mixing at home. It turned out well, and our chief course tutor Dave Ellis put his hand in his pocket to get a hundred copies pressed (or burnt or whatever you do with CDs). Not long afterwards we were invited to a meeting with college management at which we received a major bollocking for doing it. No, nor do I, but as far as I know there is still a box full of them doing nothing at Blackburn College, so if you want one…

NB: There's a 'PS' to this delightful little comedy because having inspired the making of the track in the first place Radio Lancashire refused to play it unless we signed all the rights of the record over to the BBC. You probably *could* make it up but there's no need.

It was around this time that I suddenly had another one of Darrel's 'cognisences'. We were on our way to pick Clay up from the Wirral and I was sat in traffic in Liverpool (in the car, obviously) ruminating about music when it hit me – most so-called music isn't music at all. It's noise. Horrible noise, some of it, some of it very nice, but noise nonetheless. Only a small percentage of it counts as 'music' because only a small percentage of it contains any humanity.

This is hard to explain so bear with me. People can get together, pick some songs and play them on instruments while someone else sings them (or not). If the people are musicians and the singer can sing it can sound OK, if the musicians and singer are terrific it can sound ace, but the whole process can be entirely mechanical – just, you know, get the chords right, get the sound right, get the words right and off we go. This, I reckon, is most 'music'.

Real music, music without the inverted commas, is a different ball game. This involves everyone giving themselves 100% to the piece they're playing, thus capturing the heart, soul and atmosphere of the piece while expressing themselves truly and honestly so that other human beings can feel it. And how often does that happen? Usually it's like that old joke about the muck in the sea at Blackpool, you know the one, 'you can't swim in the sea at Blackpool any more, you can only go through the motions'. Usually it's just going through the motions. Unfortunately this is purely subjective, but it's real important to me.

Point of interest – I reckon the feel of a piece of music has a profound effect on mood. I've certainly found that particular feels – swing, shuffle, a good 12/8 – lift the spirit, whereas straight-eight rock can feel just a tad aggressive. In fact it's almost the point of metal, if the poses that go with it are anything to go by. This may not show up so much in isolation, one track at a time, but how about the cumulative effect? We now live in a world that is almost exclusively straight-eight (or even straight-four if you include the compulsory 'thump thump thump thump' stuff) and not just in rock, but dance and disco and hip-hop too, and I don't sense much spirit-lifting going on. Do you? It's about time someone did a thesis on that, I think. Now where do you find a tame psychologist when you need one?

Anyway, as the parking facilities at Blackburn College went from iffy to virtually impossible I decided to leave the car at home and take the train instead, but I needed something to read on the way. I'd been promising myself for years that before I died I'd have a real go at Shakespeare, so I bought a Penguin copy of 'Hamlet' (the one with all the explanations at the back) and didn't stop reading it, on and off the train, for the next five years.

It was, and is, the greatest thing I've ever seen, read, heard, felt or tasted. Beyond genius. Incredible. Of course it is, it's *'Hamlet'* for fuck's sake, but I wasn't prepared for how phenomenal it was. If you asked me for the best piece of advice I could possibly give you it would be 'buy a Penguin copy of Hamlet'. No, really, do it. Best fiver I ever spent. Seriously.

Have you done it yet? Well what are you waiting for?

At about the same time I stumbled upon another Bill - Hicks, this time, for my money the only performer in the last thirty years who mattered, and he changed my life. Not that I could do what he did or anything like it, but he alone among performers told the truth and told it without props or lasers or fear. Rock and pop performers harbour the notion that they are rebels or revolutionaries but those days are long gone. Rock and pop now are so 'establishment' they make 'The Shipping Forecast' look ground-breaking and Bill knew it. 'Government-approved rock 'n' roll' he called it, and who wants that? But then Bill made everyone else seem 'government approved' in comparison to himself, and he made me feel totally inadequate and humble in the process.

What had I ever done that came close to his attacks on hypocrisy, injustice, cruelty, bullshit? How brave had I ever been? How far above the parapet had I ever stuck my worthless nut? He was saying what I had always been thinking – and more – and saying it loud without any of the usual 'please like me' stuff that everybody else wallowed in. Indeed when he was on the case on stage he didn't seem to care whether people liked him or not, liked his message or not. He was telling it like he saw it, he was making people (most of the people anyway) laugh at it at the same time, and he was right.

That was the killer for me, he was always right. About politics, the military, capitalism, drugs, religion, booze, pornography, smoking, he was right, and right with no apology and no watering-down. In the movie 'Bad Day at Black Rock' Spencer Tracey tells Ernest Borgnine 'you're not only wrong, you're wrong at the top of your voice'. Well Bill was right at the top of his voice and the rest of us should be ashamed. Comedy may be 'the new rock 'n' roll' but most of it's as mainstream as rock 'n' roll too. Bill's wasn't. If Hendrix was 'the black Elvis', then Bill was the comedic Hendrix and I miss him.

NB: When I told Shirle I was going to show a Bill DVD to the students at college she said 'oh, be careful, the management won't like that'. Which, of course, was precisely the point.

Meanwhile, back in college, I had arrived, via the old deductive reasoning ploy, at a few critical observations regarding what works musically and what don't. Remember I said I would bore you with phrasing? Here it is, and a few other things too.

Firstly, it's vital to understand intervals. They're the musical equivalent of letters – letters make words, intervals make tunes, but there's only 12 intervals so it's not complicated. When you sing a tune, you're singing intervals. To play a tune all you have to do is recognise its intervals and know where they are on your instrument.

Second, it's vital to be able to hear chord sequences. You don't necessarily have to be able to explain it or theorise it (remember Geoff the pianist?) but you need to understand them deep down. This is not particularly difficult as most chord sequences work on a couple of basic principles.

Thirdly you have to realise that there is no such thing as a 'wrong note'. A favourite trick of mine was to get someone to play every note on the top E string of the guitar in order, up and down, while I played the chord sequence to 'Sweet Georgia Brown' in G. It works. How can there be a 'wrong' note? Try it, it's fun.

Fourthly, don't leave gaps between notes. It's easy to do on the guitar, leaving those tiny silences, but eliminating them makes the difference between 'some bloke playing the guitar' and 'music'. I got that tip from hearing Frank Sinatra talk about Tommy Dorsey, and it gives lines on the bottom strings power and makes lines on the top ones sing. Simple.

And fifthly, phrasing. I used to read things like 'oh, it's his phrasing that makes him so special' without knowing what phrasing was, but it really is what separates the men from the boys. It's essentially the finer points of timing, and it works like comic timing does – get it spot on and you're effective, don't and you ain't. If you've ever wondered why Hank Marvin and Duane Eddy are so effective just playing tunes (and if you haven't, why not?) the answer is that their playing is gapless and perfectly phrased. And thereby endeth the lesson. The collection follows immediately.

NB: The same is true of singers too. The thing the greats have in common – Elvis Presley, Ray Charles, Frank Sinatra, Michael Jackson, Dolly Parton – is superb phrasing. They swing. It's not really about 'the voice' at all. Louis Armstrong didn't have a 'great voice, nor did Jimmy Durante, but listen to them sing! Billy Holiday, one of the best 'singers' ever, had just over an octave range, and the two best versions of Stephen Sondheim's 'Send in the Clowns' I ever heard were by Glynis Johns and Judi Dench, neither of whom are singers at all.

Speaking of singers propels me into another myth that has plagued all of us for years and seems destined to go on doing it, namely that however well you sing and/or play you're worthless unless you write your own material. This idea is so ingrained in our minds that I've been told by music students that Elvis Presley and Frank Sinatra were somehow sub-standard because they didn't write their own songs. 'You can't mean a song unless you wrote it yourself' I was told by one student. Who could, incidentally, neither sing, play or write anything worth hearing.

This myth started because of the Beatles, of course, 'the first pop stars to write their own material' but it's wrong on two counts. One, they weren't the first. Elvis and Jerry Lee Lewis may not have written their own material, but Chuck Berry did, so did Little Richard and so did Buddy Holly. And two, the Beatles *didn't* write a lot of their earlier material, they took it from other people's records. *Which was how they learned to write their own.*

The result of this myth is, of course, that everyone now writes songs, most of which are bloody awful. Back in the day great songwriters wrote great songs that singers like Elvis and Sinatra could sing better than anyone else, result: great records. If they had written their own songs the chances are they would have been crap, result: crap records. Well-sung crap, perhaps, but crap anyway. We wanted great records, sung by great singers, and fuck who wrote them.

More to the point, the 'must write your own material' myth simply doesn't hold water – no one slags off the London Symphony Orchestra or the Amadeus String Quartet because they don't write their own material, because everyone knows that Mozart and Stravinsky wrote better stuff than members of the LSO or the ASQ could throw together between them. Well, sorry chaps, but it's a fair bet that Leiber & Stoller, Cole Porter and Lennon & McCartney wrote better songs than you can. It doesn't mean you shouldn't try, but I spent thirteen years listening to students' original songs and I only came across one student who could write good ones.

Hit ones? Search me. No one knows what a hit song is until it's a hit, and even then you can't tell why. That's the magic of it, it makes no sense. You can write songs all your life, good ones, and never get a sniff of a hit, while people like Willie Nelson and Bob Dylan seemed to have diarrhoea of them. There's no rhyme or reason to it (well, there's rhyme, obviously, but… you know what I mean).

One more thing about myths before I move on – the whole point about myths is that they're mythical, and some myths are so mythical it's impossible to understand how some people can myth the point completely. For example, there's a myth that if you play an instrument you need an electronic tuner to tune it, but that's obviously bollocks because we've been tuning instruments perfectly well for millennia without them, thank you very much. If anyone asks me if I've got a tuner I say 'yes, two – one on each side of my head'.

Ah, but to tune an instrument properly you need a reference, you say. Hang on a minute, I'll write you one. Yes you do, but there's a technological development that puts tuners to shame. It's made of tempered steel so it'll survive the third world war (you won't, but it will), it's unwaveringly accurate, it's the size and weight of a pair of nail scissors, if you hold it over the pickup of an electric guitar the whole band can hear it, it's a fraction the price of an electronic tuner, the batteries never wear out and (here's the best bit) you use it to tune with your ears, not your eyes. Brilliant or what? Now *that's* modern technology for you. Well it was in 1711.

The last time I bought one it inspired the weirdest reaction I've ever had in a shop. I asked the bloke if he had any tuning forks, he said he did and asked which note I wanted. I told him I wanted a G. '*GEEEE*'? he said, his voice wavering over about three octaves in shock and disbelief – it was like I'd asked him for a Z sharp. 'Yes' I said, 'they come in twelve notes and I want one of them, what's wrong with that'? He asked me what I wanted it for, and when I told him it was for tuning a guitar he told me guitarists used either A or E. I told him G was better (it is, believe me, I won't go into it now) and before he could tell me I was wrong I gave him £8, grabbed my G tuning fork and left. Get one. Preferably a G, and you can get a few sets of strings with the money you save.

There's another myth that says you can learn to play an instrument using tab (short for tablature, a system that shows you where to put your fingers on the frets) but that is plainly bollocks too, because music goes in through your ears, not your eyes. Would you learn to paint by ear? I think not.

And another thing – who started this 'drummer counting in by going click click click' jazz? They all do it now and it's insane. For a start it's not the drummer's job to dictate the tempo, and anyway it works far better through the mouth because when you count in that way you also indicate the feel of the piece. More significantly – *far* more significantly – if you miss someone shouting 'one...' or even 'one, two...'

you can still hear 'three, four…' and come in. If you miss a click you're fucked, as the next wee tale will illustrate.

When I was with Steely at the Adelphi, most of the show featured 'live' vocals. But there was one piece – a medley of old London songs – that required Tom to do a full dance routine with his dancers, and for this the vocals were pre-recorded and fed to the MD (Peter Collins) through cans, preceded by four clicks so he could cue the band. Well, one night Pete only got three clicks in his cans, which meant the band were a beat behind the vocals. Now, with a trio or quartet you could simply jump a beat, but a twenty-odd piece band is a bit like an oil tanker – slow to react – so Pete's only option was to conduct the band faster than the vocal track in an attempt to catch up. Fine, you say, but… like an oil tanker, when the band catches up it's going too fast and overtakes the vocal, which means… well you know what it means.

Consequently, Tom and the dancers were trying to dance – in time with the vocals – while twenty-odd people behind them were speeding up and slowing down like a boat on a rolling sea. It was impossible, clearly, and at the time the effect was so ridiculous that while felt terrible for Tom I could hardly play for laughing. How the 'blowers' in the band managed I've no idea. Naturally Tom went absolutely fucking ballistic afterwards, not at the band but at the sound man who had started the recording one click late. *But…* and here's the point… if that count-in had been a 'one, two, three, four…' count, through the mouth, missing the 'one' wouldn't have mattered, would it? Yet every band you see has the drummer going 'click, click, click'. Why?

All these myths – *all* myths – are easily consigned to the khazi of derision if you think them through, so why are we not thinking them through? You know, someone once said that when a man stops believing in God he doesn't believe in nothing, he'll believe *anything*. Maybe that's it.

Where was I? Oh aye, back at college Wednesday evening was band rehearsal time and for a few years I manned the rehearsal rooms and helped the bands out as and when necessary. One year, however, we had a few guitarists who weren't in bands, so I commandeered a classroom and started running weekly 'tune-playing' sessions with them, using material like 'Eleanor Rigby' and 'You Only Live Twice' and coaching them pretty much by ear. When we first started it could take a full evening to get a tune together, but the learning curve was so steep that by the second year we were adding, and arranging, a new tune every *hour,* and stretching the old complexity envelope to include things like 'Angel Eyes', real harmonic stuff.

The stars of this group were people like Curtis Gould, Ash Philips and the aforementioned Jordan Westwell, with Greg Harper adding his two-pennyworth on bass. The results spoke for themselves and it was the best fun I think any of us had ever had on the course as well as proving to be by far the best learning tool.

Bearing that in mind, our course had, for the previous few years, been sort-of taken over by an outside company who claimed they were the largest private music tuition organisation in the world. We had to implement their material along with our own and they moderated the course overall too, making their presence powerfully felt. The trouble was that their material was no better than the old course stuff and arguably a damned sight worse.

The students certainly didn't care for it much and I was loath, frankly, to impose it on them at all as I was certain it would do nothing to make them more effective musicians. This company's material consisted of eight grades, but we usually only used the first six because seven and eight were, in my opinion, too difficult and even more pointless.

Anyway, at the beginning of one year we took receipt of a new student who, all on his own, had already achieved grade eight with this company and had been within two marks of a distinction to boot. Fab going, you may say. And so it came to pass that one evening he walked in on one of our Wednesday sessions, listened for a while, and then announced to everybody concerned that he had no clue about what was going on.

The man who had already achieved the company's highest grade could make nothing of 'You Only Live Twice', 'Eleanor Rigby' or any of the other tunes we were playing, and thereby hangs the tale. It seems to me that everybody is benefitting from co-called music education except the students, who end up as nothing more than cash cows for someone else's financial benefit. Sorry if I sound a little angry about this. I'm not angry actually. I'm fucking *incandescent*. Still, you've got to laugh, eh?

Trying to come up with a concrete theme for our Wednesday night bashes I suggested we form a 'guitar choir' that the students could take and use to create something lasting and, hopefully, profitable. It wasn't the best idea in the world but it was something. But it came to nothing for the same old reason – a built-in 'what's the point, it won't work' feeling that permeated the group, as it had permeated every other group I'd ever been involved with.

It's an English thing, the same thing that stops us from enjoying ourselves or producing (at the time of writing) a Wimbledon men's champion. There's something missing, a bit of us we can't reach, a bit that Bjorn Borg, Pete Sampras and Roger Federer *could* reach and Tim Henman couldn't, the same bit that musicians of every other nationality seem to be able to reach but us, the same bit that leaves English people unable to judge music for themselves. It's like a mental disability, but institutional. Deliberate. Like we've been brainwashed. Which of course we have.

Like anything else, once you've seen it you see it everywhere and you realise it's so deeply ingrained there's nothing you can do but weep. Those Eton students proved the point for me because they don't have the problem, it's never been ingrained in them that they don't matter and are doomed to fail. The rest of us have been taught to know our place, do as we're told or else, and we've lost our hearts in the process. They're still there, deep down, we're human after all, but we can't reach them. Then we wonder why people take drugs or get pissed or riot. I only wonder why more people don't.

261

Bizarrely, it was during a break preceding these evening sessions that I idly typed 'winter bathing' into the office computer and I literally stopped breathing. There they were in all their glory, deep snow, thick ice, minus 20 or 30 and they're stripped off and frolicking in the freezing water, hundreds of 'em in half a dozen different countries, and clearly loving it. I didn't show it outwardly but inside I was screaming like a 14-year-old girl at a pop concert. I couldn't have been more envious if I'd had an NVQ in envy from the 'Lucky Bastards' faculty of the University of Jealousy, Green Land.

Those clips had a profound effect on me because they told me that what I'd read fifty years ago was right, that ice-breaking wasn't a rare form of insanity but a popular and widespread recreation, that it could be far more extreme than I'd ever imagined and that my own innate reactions were perfectly valid. I was simply in the wrong place. Only in England is it regarded (if it's regarded at all) as a perversion practised by a handful of nutters. Had I been born in Finland or Sweden or Denmark or Poland or Russia I'd simply have been invited to join in.

Of course I tried to imagine what it was like, but as I've never experienced anything like minus 20, with or without clothes, it was impossible. You know, some fortunate countries get lovely warm summers followed by crisp, frosty winters. English winters are kind-of like our summers – just as wet but a bit colder and with less hours of daylight. 'Everything else in England might be shit, but at least you can rely on the weather' I always say.

But then fate played its hand – for two winters on the trot we got a couple of really cold snaps (more minus 10 than minus 20 but sub-zero at least) and a decent fall of snow to go with it. It didn't last long, and I couldn't manage the real McCoy (no place, no contacts) but I found a secluded spot in the garden, filled some buckets with water, loaded it up with snow to get the temperature right down, stripped off and... well, I don't have to draw you a picture, do I? If I did you wouldn't like it – I can't draw.

How did it feel? Like paradise. Like being kissed awake by angels. And I learned a vital lesson in the process – the more frozen you get the more sensational it feels. It's impossible to explain, but freezing ain't simply cold times ten, it's as different as warm water is from boiling (though I wouldn't suggest bathing in that). It thrills you to begin with and then becomes positively euphoric so you end up feeling more alive than you ever felt before, and that's just with some buckets at minus 10. Fuck knows how it feels to bathe in it at minus 20 or 30, or swim in water that's 1.8 degrees below freezing, but deductive reasoning, based on my comparatively tentative experiments, suggests that it feels fucking *amazing* Watson.

On one of those crisp, snowy days Iain Reddy and I took a walk around Rowley Lake in Burnley. It's one of those places you can't quite credit – almost in the town centre yet somehow miles from anywhere and a beautiful place for a stroll on a warm summer's day, but English winters being what they are I didn't think I would ever see it frozen. Well, it was frozen that day and it looked... well, like Finland, and

I swear I could sense ghostly voices beckoning me to 'come on in, the water's lovely'. It was out of the question, of course, but I've never felt more bereft. What was I in a past life, a fucking penguin?

NB: Some people have asked me why I've never just hopped on a plane and tried it. Well, for one thing, it's pricey. Places like Finland and Denmark are expensive, to visit and stay in, especially if you don't know anyone, and I never had the wherewithal. Secondly, you can't just go blundering in to a thing like that – you'd need a little mentoring to start with, and like I said I don't know anyone. And thirdly, I'm certain that if I went and tried it I'd want to keep doing it forever, and then what? Come *home*? Can you imagine?

Blackburn College eventually fired me after thirteen years for being too old. They had asked me if I wanted to keep working when I reached 65, I said I did and I was told the management were perfectly happy for me to do so. Then the college heard that the government was bringing in anti-age discrimination laws in a few months' time, and decided that since they wouldn't be able to discriminate against me after that they would do it before the legislation kicked in.

There was no warning, no preamble, no discussion, no attempt to justify the decision and no right of appeal, much less any of that 'last in, first out' bollocks. We've decided you should piss off so piss off, is what it amounted to. I stormed out in disgust and got pissed on the way home. These are the ways of our education system and it's a fucking disgrace. John Ridgeon, incidentally, had sold Access to

Music a few years earlier, sick of the paperwork and politics. These are the ways of our education system and it's a fucking disgrace.

NB: Incidentally, when Dave Ellis and I did the CertEd course, as commanded, we were instructed to read as much as we could about education, especially the work of Carl Rogers who was rated the No 1 education philosopher in the education firmament. As Dave and I were both working pretty constantly we had little time for such reading, but I did Google 'Carl Rogers' to find out what I could, and I came across a quote of his which read roughly thus: 'Once I discovered what education was really all about I felt obliged to give it up'. When I mentioned this to one of our CertEd tutors he ignored me. 'But surely…' I said, but he'd gone.

As it happens by the time I got fired I'd arrived at the same conclusion as old Carl, at least as far as music was concerned, so maybe it was time for me to follow in his footsteps. The only thing that sticks in my craw (is that a real word, 'craw'? Must be I suppose) is that by simply walking out I'd done nothing to address all my concerns about the course and its students. Still, you've got to laugh, eh?

Following my departure Greg Harper, God bless him, set about getting as much of me on YouTube as possible as well as setting me up a website of my own. I didn't have a computer at the time – I reckon technology is the spawn of Satan so I deliberately avoided it – but it sort of made sense once I was out of work so I succumbed and bought an 'enchanted tea-tray'. I'm writing this on it now, as it happens, and I've downloaded some of those winter bathing clips too, so it's not all bad.

My final act (to date) was kind of apposite to the writing of this tale 'cause it celebrated my 50th year in music. I called it my '50th anniversary one-gig tour' and we staged it at a delightful little theatre in Darwen. I wasn't planning to do it at all, to be honest, but I hadn't played a gig in a while and dear old Greg browbeat me into it. 'It's a great little theatre' he said, 'you'll love it'.

So I jotted down some songs I wouldn't mind doing, wrote a few originals and called a few people. Iain Reddy, Ken Bradshaw, Liam Barber, Curtis Gould and a fine jazz singer called Gloria Hoole all said 'yes', Liam brought along boogie piano specialist Justin Randall, Greg tracked down Jordan Westwell and we were set. As I wanted the night to sound fresh I refused all demands to rehearse, and we decided that any profit we made would go to the Wirral Autistic Society.

I intended to use the week before the gig to get myself match-fit (diet, bit of exercise, you know) but... and you absolutely *knew* there would be a 'but' coming, right?... in the true 'up & down' spirit of the bride's nightie the bad news hit like a train. Five days before the gig Clay was rushed to intensive care and it didn't look good. I spent the next five days living on fags and vodka, by the night of the gig we were fielding phone calls from the Wirral and just praying for the best, and I did the gig purely on those fifty years of experience. It was a bit of a triumph if I do say so myself, for the band and the audience alike; in fact it worked better than

I could possibly have hoped and I couldn't have been prouder of, or more grateful to, everyone involved, but for me the night was a trifle overshadowed by Clay.

On that topic, I realise that most of my overpowering and perennial sense of guilt comes from having a good Catholic education, but where kids are concerned I believe the subject to be much more cut and dried. Some people seem to think their kids owe them something for bringing them up, but for me it's the other way round.

Our kids wouldn't be here but for us, wouldn't have to suffer the slings and arrows of outrageous fortune but for our doings, and since I lumbered Clay with his mortal existence, with all that that entails, I'm the guilty party. Deductive reasoning, see? Everything that happens to him is down to me, good or bad, so when it's bad (and he's never had it easy) it's my fault.

Epilogue...

Whatever Darwin thought, and for reasons he would probably never have even imagined, we English are de-evolving. As you will have gathered if you've read this far, I've played in just about every kind of environment from makeshift stages to the Victoria Palace, working men's clubs to the concert arena, and the one thing that's clear to me is that we have un-learnt along the way.

Popular entertainment, for want of a better phrase, started in pubs and clubs but evolved rapidly during the late 1890s and early 20th century into the kind of palaces designed by Frank Matcham, wondrous places that were not only breath-taking to look at but presented their entertainments in the best possible light – every seat in the house had a perfect view of the stage, and the acoustics were good enough to allow unamplified singers and comedians to be heard by everyone in the audience.

Since then we have pulled almost all of them down and replaced them with... what, exactly? A handful of fine concert venues certainly, like the Barbican and the Bridgewater Hall, and... what? Well, fuck all essentially. Most of us have been forced back to the pubs and clubs the theatres evolved from, and if that ain't de-evolution I'd like to know what is.

Some beautiful local theatres were even pulled down and replaced with 'multi-purpose' places, basically huge concrete boxes with sports lines on the floor and a stage in one side, OK for the sports, maybe, but as much use as a fishnet condom for performance, with bad visibility and acoustics like an underground car park.

Now, as anyone who's ever worked them will tell you, pubs and clubs are the worst places imaginable to play in. The people who run them often don't give a fuck about the act or the band, the stages are either tiny or non-existent, and the audiences are usually pissed. Consequently only the loudest, brashest 'turns' survive while real talent falleth on stony ground. The last places anyone should perform is in a pub or a club, but they're almost all there is and that's plain destructive.

I hate to labour the point, but... when we started back in the 1950s we started with skiffle, which effectively meant strumming a few simple chords badly while someone sang. We evolved from this through the Shadows, the Beatles and the Who to Cream and, ultimately, Jimi Hendrix, all featuring increasingly adventurous and inventive musicianship.

If you watch almost any band now you will see that what they're playing is, effectively, skiffle. The songs may have changed, but the musicians are strumming a few simple chords while someone sings. And if *that* ain't de-evolution I'd like to know what is. Yes, I know music now is brilliant and amazing, much better than all that old Beatles/Mozart shit, but what next?

I said I didn't make friends easily when I was a kid. Well, it didn't stop there. I've never made friends easily because, like most Englishmen, I always had to be right, and you know how bloody annoying *that* is.

I can justify it, of course I can. I was told so often that I was wrong – about the house in Hornsey, about school, about music, about ice-breakers, about not being a real soldier, about just about everything – that I felt obliged to over-compensate by over-justifying myself, if that makes any semantic sense, and by feeling obliged to justify every decision I became good at it, which means that very often I *was* right.

This, however, came at a cost, because having to be right all the time makes everyone else feel obliged to prove you wrong whether you're right or not, and that's just plain bloody frustrating for everyone. I can only apologise. I really would love to have been a diamond geezer but you can only play the hand you're dealt.

Of course that's not the only reason I find it hard to make friends. Truth is I've spent so much time on my own, pondering the meaning of life and the details thereof, that when I meet someone my opening gambit ain't 'how's the wife and kids' but 'man, have you seen Al Pacino's film about Richard III' or some such art-related topic. I can't help this any more than I can help being five foot six but it places my social skills on the 'special needs' end of the scale.

What's interesting, not to mention infuriating, is to be suddenly exposed to the opposite end of the spectrum, the 'he never met a stranger' end. I did a gig once for CAMRA, the organisation that campaigns for real ale, and after setting up my gear I went backstage to find our bass player, Bert Edwards, chatting with the three blokes that organised the event like he'd known them for years. I could no more have done that than fly to Jupiter and set up a guest house, unless the three blokes involved had just seen Al Pacino's film about Richard III.

Likewise, I never 'hung around' with the lads after a gig or a session, bought rounds of drinks and chatted about nothing. I went home. Now anyone will tell you that the biggest favour you can do yourself is to 'be a great bloke' but I couldn't. I don't know how. I never learned. Don't get me wrong, I don't think I'm an arsehole either. I'll never do you harm on purpose, I just don't have what it takes to be a great bloke. For me it's always been about the work, period. 'Love my playing, love me' sort of thing. And if you don't, you won't.

Bizarrely, my need to be right all the time is the only English thing about me. In every other way I couldn't be less English if I'd been born in space. I hate conformity and queuing, I'm essentially left wing (in fact I get more Marxist the older I get), I'm far from philistine, I can judge music for myself and I don't like football. Most significantly, perhaps, I don't think 'this is still the best country in the world', possibly because I've actually seen some others. And all the things I crave – jazz, rock 'n' roll, winter bathing, passion, joy – are somewhere else.

I have a soft spot for the language, the breakfasts and the BBC, but I really could do without the moaning. Having said that, though, we do have an inordinate amount to moan about, and if we didn't moan about it we'd just seem apathetic. God, there's a tin of worms I've opened, eh?

271

Perhaps the point is that we moan about things because we're English, but we don't do anything to correct them because we're English.

I always say that if you want to sum England up in one word, try 'Titanic'. It's a brilliant feat of engineering and definitely not sinkable. No way. Not under any circumstances. Not the way we've designed it. Yes, we're putting lifeboats on it, obviously, even though it's definitely unsinkable. We're just not putting *enough* lifeboats on it because it doesn't really need any and it would spoil the look. We are putting enough lifeboats on it for the rich passengers, obviously, even though it's quite unnecessary, and we will be carrying binoculars for the lookouts though they will be locked away in the binocular cupboard to stop anyone nicking them. But don't worry, they won't be needed because whatever happens it's unsinkable. What? Oh.

NB: The final English stamp on the Titanic cock-up is one I only found out about recently, namely that the White Star Line stopped paying the crew's wages the moment the ship went down on the grounds that 'they weren't working on it any more'. Not even a week's notice, you'll notice. How English can you get?

Or try the word 'Somme'. OK, lads, we've been ordered by our superiors to get up out of our trenches and walk slowly across no-man's land towards the heavily-fortified German machine gun emplacements. It sounds reckless I grant you, not to mention insane, pointless and suicidal, but we've been ordered to do it by our superiors back in London and we must obey their orders without question. I'd rather not, obviously, the 'reckless, insane, pointless and suicidal' aspects bother me a bit, but I know my place and our superiors hundreds of miles away in Blighty must know what they're doing. What? Oh.

'To be successful in our profession is sometimes as simple as being in the right place at the right time. Sadly this is not as easy as it sounds'. That, I think, is one of the funniest lines I ever read and also one of the most profound. Eric Sykes wrote it in his autobiography 'If I Don't Write it Nobody Else Will' and it's spot bollock.

Many people attribute success to luck. I don't. I attribute it to fate, and if you've read as many biographies and autobiographies as I have you'll agree with me. How often have you heard a major star say 'well, it all started with a phone call out of the blue'? No one ever 'planned' their success. They may have planned 'for' it, but when it came it was inevitably 'out of the blue'. If you really want convincing, a thorough reading of the Beatles story should do it for you 'cause you couldn't make that up. J K Rowling couldn't make it up.

Some people say you can achieve anything you set your mind on but you can't, you know. I've known plenty of people, good people, talented people, who have put everything into perfecting whatever skills they possess and achieved fuck all. Brilliant, some of them, and they've achieved nothing because fate decreed they should achieve nothing. I also know, and so do you, plenty of people with no discernible talent at all who have become household names. You're picturing a couple now, aren't you? Be honest.

In a real sense this doesn't matter because the great creator Richard Dawkins... no, wait a minute, not Richard Dawkins... GOD, that's the chap, has planned it that way and He knows what He's doing. And what we call 'achievement' is a very tenuous concept anyway, based (as it usually is) on sales figures and ratings. Based on sales figures and ratings, heroin is hugely successful, EastEnders is better than Hamlet and Westlife are bigger than the Beatles. The only time 'achievement' matters is when 'achievers' claim all the credit for themselves (the 'I'm a self-made man' brigade) and in fairness most great artists and performers don't. Because they know it all started with a phone call out of the blue.

Of course I realise the concept of fate is out of fashion because 'fate' implies some sort of guiding hand and we're all atheists now. But there's a problem with atheism that I don't think atheists have quite grasped, namely that it's bollocks.

I always say that anyone who doubts the existence of God simply isn't paying attention, and I'll say it again if you like. But the trouble with devout atheists is that they behave exactly the same way they condemn other people for behaving, namely taking a fundamentalist stance and telling anyone who doesn't agree with them that they're wrong. And not just wrong, but insane, stupid or deluded. OK, they don't blow up trains for their beliefs, but they wouldn't, would they, as they don't believe in anything.

I'm a Christian and I have no problem with Judaism, Islam, Hinduism or any other faith. Nor do I have a problem with science or evolution. This is because I have an open mind and I'm capable of rational thought. Anyone who calls a few billion religious followers insane, stupid or deluded has clearly shut his mind tighter than a duck's arse, awarded himself a Nobel Prize in arrogance and given up thinking for Lent, and if that ain't a fundamentalist stance…

Let me give you one little example and I'll move on. OK? OK, then. The last time scientists examined the Turin Shroud, which has long been believed to be the winding sheet of Jesus Christ, they examined it in order to prove it a fake, a forgery. Well let's face it, it is the most logical conclusion, because if it ain't a fake it's a 2000-year-old photograph and that's impossible. So they subjected it to every scientific test known to man and ended up proving it genuine. It is a 2000-year-old photograph of Jesus Christ.

Now, having proved it genuine – or, if you like, failed to prove it a fake or a forgery – the logical, open-minded response would be to say 'well we don't understand it but…' But scientists didn't say that. Despite it being proved kosher by their fellow scientists, scientists said it couldn't be, so it isn't. Now shoot me down in flames if I err, but isn't that just a tad closed-minded? Scientists say that science is about investigation, but how can that be when they refuse to accept the results of their own investigations because it conflicts with their beliefs? Isn't that almost the definition of 'fundamentalism'?

OK, enough of that, I just wanted to make the point that musicians are generally aware of the numinous because they have talent they can't explain, get inspiration from somewhere they can't describe and can sense things like timing, phrasing, swing, groove, tone and expression that science can't prove, explain or reproduce under laboratory conditions. And they know about fate, too, if they ever got one of those phone calls or read about the Beatles.

Asked how he wrote his songs, John Lennon once said 'I don't know who writes them, all I know is when I need them they come'. And Brian Wilson said 'I take no credit for the songs I wrote with the Beach Boys because I was always aware of a higher power there with me when I was writing them'. As I said, musicians are aware of the numinous, and that makes us very fortunate indeed.

Now what did I come in here for, Oh yes. We hear so much these days about 'old people' we seem to forget that things have changed since 1945. Back in the 50s old people really did seem to be from another generation. They wore *their* clothes, listened to *their* music, got *their* haircuts, proclaimed *their* attitudes, none of which had any relevance for us.

But old people these days – old people my age at least – are the beat generation. We're the ones who invented rock 'n' roll, blue jeans, electric guitars, drugs, sex and teenagers. It was us who made stars of Elvis and the Beatles, us who started everything you take for granted, so before you start patronising us get your hair cut and go tidy your room.

Yes, I know, we're responsible for the society you've inherited and for that we should be deeply ashamed. I know I am. I guess it just proves that however good things seem on the surface, underneath it there are bastards and idiots burrowing away like death-watch beetles in a Stradivarius. Still, mustn't grumble, eh?

So, I now find myself officially 'retired', but as you can't 'retire' from who you are it's an ambiguous point at best. 'Resting', thespians call it, but that was a dubious euphemism too. The best thing about it is that, being over 65, I am out of reach of the nice people at the JobCentre, another euphemism of Orwellian double-speak dubiousness for so, so many reasons. It means I'm reliant on a pension, but in this day and age, when young people with families are reliant on a damned sight less, I ain't complaining.

But no, of course you can't 'retire' when the purpose of your life is to become as good and informed a musician as you can be, and in that sense I won't stop for several thousand years yet. I've still got plenty of weaknesses that need addressing, thanks very much. I still can't play with the depth of expression I should, still don't have a tone as good as Hank's, still can't improvise like Wes, still can't play slide guitar like Ry Cooder or fingerpick like Chet, and there's a thousand years each there for a start.

As for guitars, I'm still as obsessed with them as I ever was, probably more, and clinically unable to survive without one for more than an hour or two. I once made a serious error in judgement when ATM asked me to direct student bands at a weekend summer school, and assuming the bands would be doing all the playing I didn't take a guitar with me. I got there on the Friday evening, and by Saturday morning I was in such a state of withdrawal I was running around begging to borrow one like a junkie in a crack house.

I'm still reading, and listening too. You know, the better you get as a musician the more you can hear in other people's music. I'm aware of things now I wasn't aware of ten years ago, and while I've lost patience with a lot of mediocre music as a result, I recognise greatness in ways I never thought possible and that's truly joyful. Perhaps now when I get my final gig in the great eternal concert hall and find Elvis on vocals, Mozart on keyboards and Hendrix on guitar I'll at least be fit to play rhythm guitar for them.

You know, some people expect to get to paradise when they die but not me. I've done nothing to deserve it so why should I? But there's an old song that runs 'I'm gonna walk and talk with Jesus some of these days' and that would be nice, wouldn't it? To actually meet the guvnor?

Woody Allen famously said he wasn't afraid of death, he just didn't want to be there when it happened. I just hope I die before Richard Dawkins so I get to see the look on his face when he arrives.

Ladies & gentlemen, please put your hands together for...

The No 1 piece of advice in the days of variety was 'always finish on a song'. This advice was considered somewhat superfluous by most singers, but was adopted by comics and worked, I'm assured, rather well. Obviously I can't finish on a song here – well I could but you wouldn't be able to hear me. So in lieu of that I thought I'd finish on a poem instead. Yes, I occasionally write those too, though they usually end up as lyrics. This one didn't (well, you try to come up with a tune for it) but it seems to sum up all that has gone before only more succinctly. The poem's called 'Fit For the Job' and I can only add:

Thank you, you've been a wonderful audient, and if you've enjoyed reading this half as much as I've enjoyed writing it then I've enjoyed it twice as much as you have.

I'm here all week.

Tone

FIT FOR THE JOB

Why did you make me so shit, Lord? Why did you make me so lame?

Sorry for sounding ungrateful but there's nobody else I can blame.

Why did you not make me perfect? Tall, dark and handsome and strong,

With genitals like a rhinoceros, would it have really been wrong?

Why did you not give me genius? Or charm? Or charisma? Or grace?

Or courage? Or good DIY skills? Would it have been out of place?

Why did you never inspire me to write a hit novel or tune?

Or to stick a dead shark in formaldehyde, would it be asking the moon?

You must understand at this juncture, it's not for myself I complain,

But being a failure fails everyone else, and that's what's tormenting my brain.

So why did you make me so shit, Lord? So ineffectual a knob?

I could have been such a great geezer if you'd made me fit for the job.

<u>FIN</u>

Printed in Great Britain
by Amazon

30569698R00160